CAMBRIDGE LIBRARY COLLECTION

Books of enduring scholarly value

East and South-East Asian History

This series focuses on East and South-East Asia from the early modern period to the end of the Victorian era. It includes contemporary accounts of European encounters with the civilisations of China, Japan and South-East Asia from the time of the Jesuit missions and the East India companies to the Chinese revolution of 1911.

Desultory Notes on the Government and People of China, and on the Chinese Language

Inspired by the lectures in Munich of the German orientalist Karl Friedrich Neumann, Thomas Taylor Meadows (1815–68) devoted himself to the study of Chinese in 1841, with the aim of entering British service. He arrived in China early in 1843 and rose quickly to the post of consular interpreter at the key treaty port of Canton (Guangzhou), where he remained for several years. During this time, he developed a keen understanding of Chinese affairs, shrewdly cultivating an intelligence network of amenable informants. First published in 1847, this work addresses diverse topics, ranging from the difficulties in learning written and spoken Chinese, through to the nature of bureaucracy and corruption in Canton province. The book sheds light on the period and the tensions in southern China prior to the Taiping Rebellion, a subject later covered by Meadows in The Chinese and their Rebellions (1856), which is also reissued in this series.

T0384570

Cambridge University Press has long been a pioneer in the reissuing of out-of-print titles from its own backlist, producing digital reprints of books that are still sought after by scholars and students but could not be reprinted economically using traditional technology. The Cambridge Library Collection extends this activity to a wider range of books which are still of importance to researchers and professionals, either for the source material they contain, or as landmarks in the history of their academic discipline.

Drawing from the world-renowned collections in the Cambridge University Library and other partner libraries, and guided by the advice of experts in each subject area, Cambridge University Press is using state-of-the-art scanning machines in its own Printing House to capture the content of each book selected for inclusion. The files are processed to give a consistently clear, crisp image, and the books finished to the high quality standard for which the Press is recognised around the world. The latest print-on-demand technology ensures that the books will remain available indefinitely, and that orders for single or multiple copies can quickly be supplied.

The Cambridge Library Collection brings back to life books of enduring scholarly value (including out-of-copyright works originally issued by other publishers) across a wide range of disciplines in the humanities and social sciences and in science and technology.

Desultory Notes on the Government and People of China, and on the Chinese Language

Illustrated with a Sketch of the Province of Kwang-Tung, Shewing its Division into Departments and Districts

THOMAS TAYLOR MEADOWS

CAMBRIDGE
UNIVERSITY PRESS

CAMBRIDGE
UNIVERSITY PRESS

University Printing House, Cambridge, CB2 8BS, United Kingdom

Cambridge University Press is part of the University of Cambridge.
It furthers the University's mission by disseminating knowledge in the pursuit of
education, learning and research at the highest international levels of excellence.

www.cambridge.org
Information on this title: www.cambridge.org/9781108080484

This edition first published 1847
This digitally printed version 2017

ISBN 978-1-108-08048-4 Paperback

J.R.Jobbins. del.

A MANDARIN OF THE SECOND CLASS IN FULL DRESS UNIFORM: WINTER CAP

Published by W.H. Allen & C° Leadenhall Street March 1847

DESULTORY NOTES

ON

THE GOVERNMENT AND PEOPLE

OF

C H I N A,

AND ON

THE CHINESE LANGUAGE;

ILLUSTRATED WITH A

SKETCH OF THE PROVINCE OF KWANG-TÛNG,

SHEWING ITS

DIVISION INTO DEPARTMENTS AND DISTRICTS.

BY

THOMAS TAYLOR MEADOWS,

Interpreter to Her Britannic Majesty's Consulate at Canton.

LONDON:

WM. H. ALLEN AND CO.,

7, LEADENHALL STREET.

1847.

TO

ROBERT THOM, Esq.,

HER BRITANNIC MAJESTY'S CONSUL AT NING-PO,

𝕿𝖍𝖊𝖘𝖊 𝕹𝖔𝖙𝖊𝖘

ARE DEDICATED,

AS A

TESTIMONIAL OF RESPECT FOR HIS HIGH CHARACTER
AND TALENTS,

BY

HIS OBLIGED AND GRATEFUL FRIEND,

THE WRITER.

PREFACE.

THAT the reader may be enabled to form some judgment as to the degree of reliance to be placed on the statements and opinions put forth in the following Notes, I shall here shew on what grounds I found my title to write on China.

I conceive myself entitled to write on China, firstly, because I have some practical knowledge of the Chinese language; secondly, because I have bestowed my whole time and undivided attention on Chinese affairs for nearly five years; and thirdly, because, during nearly three years of that period, I have been placed in an unusually favourable position for acquiring a knowledge of those particular subjects on which I have ventured to write.

I commenced the study of the Chinese language in November, 1841, at the Royal University of Munich, with the express view of seeking a place in the service of our Government in

China. I attended the lectures of Professor
Neumann at the University during the winter
term, and almost immediately gave up every
other study I was residing in Germany to
prosecute for this one. I arrived in China in
the beginning of 1843; and in July of the same
year, on the opening of this port under the new
system, I was sent here with the late Mr. Lay
by Sir Henry Pottinger. Since that time I have
held the post of interpreter to the Consulate.
Mr. Lay understood Chinese himself; but since
his departure in June, 1844, i. e. for a period of
two years, all the Chinese business of the Consulate has necessarily been and necessarily continues to be transacted through me. To those
who are acquainted with the extent of trade at
this port, and with the multifarious duties incumbent on the Consular establishment in consequence of our treaties, this will be irrefragable
evidence that I possess some practical knowledge
of the language. Exclusive of a half-yearly number of about 2,500 printed Chinese forms connected with the reporting of ships and goods
which are issued from the Consulate, and are
filled up, &c. by me and under my superinten-

dence; and exclusive, also, of a considerable number of local proclamations on subjects connected with foreigners, which I have translated for transmission to H.M.'s Plenipotentiary at Hong-Kong, I have translated upwards of 350 official letters that have passed between the mandarins and H.M.'s Consul on a variety of special subjects. It must not be forgotten that, in addition to this, all the oral communication which has taken place in conferences with the mandarins, &c. has been kept up solely through me.

I have troubled the reader with these details because I do not conceive that any man is entitled to write on a foreign people unless he possess a practical knowledge of their language. Without this knowledge it is next to impossible that he should write any thing original about them. He may collect information from those that do know the language, and he may adopt their opinions, but he cannot form them for himself; or if he does risk it, they can scarcely have other foundation than his own imaginations. That this is the case with respect to our neighbouring countries in Europe, every one who, possessing a knowledge of the language, has lived in one of them, will admit, and will I think be ready to allow that it must be eminently the case with respect to China.

Since my arrival here I have availed myself of every opportunity that has offered to associate with Chinese, who before have had no intercourse with Europeans, with the object, which I have constantly kept in view, of making myself acquainted with the institutions and government of the country, and with the character of the people; of discovering the reasons for so many of their actions that appear very odd until these reasons are known; and of learning generally by what motives they are actuated in their conduct to us. I conceived it necessary that a government servant should obtain clear and distinct ideas on all these subjects; this could of course be best done by composing short dissertations on them, and hence the origin of these Notes.

I have reduced them to less than half their original size, by suppressing all that related to Anglo-Chinese affairs. Of the purely Chinese matters, too, this volume treats only of two kinds: of those which are nearly, or entirely, new to the

British public, as the civil divisions of the provinces, the duties and incomes of the mandarins,
and the inferior agents of government, &c.; and
of those which, though not unknown to the
public, seem to me to be regarded in an erroneous
light. I could easily have increased this volume
to thrice its present size, had I thought proper
to let the reader know for the twentieth time,
that the Chinese wear tails, and have got a cock
in the outer angle of the eye ; or had I thought
fit to corroborate what has been already said on
much more important subjects, in works too well
known and justly prized to require to be specified
here.

In treating of those subjects which seem to be
regarded in an erroneous light, it has been impossible for me to avoid alluding, in a criticising
tone, to the works of former writers—some of
them great authorities—on the same subjects. I
must, therefore, remind the reader, that a man of
inferior intellect may, favoured by his position,
ascertain facts enabling him to discover and point
out the errors of more talented people, who wrote
without a knowledge of such facts. There are
situations, too, in which a man may get a greater

insight into the feelings and characters of other
people in one hour, than he would do in a whole
year's association with them under ordinary
circumstances ; and when I inform the reader
that a British Consulate in China is a court of
law, not merely for British subjects, but also for
the Chinese, over whom the Consul has virtually
(though not nominally) considerable power, he
will understand that an interpreter must frequently be placed in such situations. He will
also be pleased to remember, that if we are deterred from criticising others by the fear of being
called presumptuous, there will be an end to
improvement of all kinds.

In justice to me, the reader will, I trust, bear
in mind, that a Note on any one subject is not a
full account of it.

I have now, in concluding, only to offer my
excuses for the frequent occurrence of the first
personal pronoun *I*, in these Notes. As they
were commenced and continued for a long time
without any immediate idea of publication, I
followed, in writing them, the most natural mode
of expression ; and though, in preparing them for
the press, I have expunged a great number of the

I's, still, as a sort of philological repugnance would not permit me to call myself *we*, they could not be altogether omitted. I must therefore be content with entreating the reader to pardon this defect, should he consider it one, in a collection of *Desultory* Notes.

T. T. M.

Canton,
June 15th, 1846.

CONTENTS.

DESULTORY NOTES

ON THE

GOVERNMENT AND PEOPLE OF CHINA,

&c.

NOTE I.

ON THE FALSE NOTIONS EXTANT IN ENGLAND REGARDING CHINA AND THE CHINESE.

THIS note I place at the commencement, by way of apology for the publication of the others, as it partly shews how much may yet be written on China, before the subject is fully understood and exhausted.

The false notions entertained with respect to China and the Chinese are very numerous. Perhaps the great reason is, that it is only during the last twelve years, since the cessation of the East-India Company's monopoly, that any number of the English people generally have had a direct interest in, or inclination to examine into, the state of the nation; while, during these twelve years, there have only been two or three persons in China, whose knowledge of the written and spoken language enabled them to get any thing like accurate information on many interesting

B

points. Through the medium of the Canton English it is literally impossible to obtain this sort of information. The Chinese who speak it are, or have been, most of them, servants ; hence they are very ignorant themselves, and the few who are well informed, feeling it quite impossible to express themselves in the only medium of communication, do not attempt it, but give any sort of vague answer which they think most likely to satisfy the European, and put an end to his inquiries. In addition to this, those who speak the Canton English seem hitherto to have made it a rule to say as little as possible to the foreigner about Chinese affairs ; they cannot see what good it will do them, and there are instances, well known to all, of some of their class having suffered severely for giving information. They take it for granted, moreover, that the " outlandish devil," although, it may be, a very good fellow, whom they would like to oblige, cannot understand the matters he inquires after, and therefore give him the same sort of vague and general answers that papa gives to a little boy, when the latter asks questions on subjects which his yet limited knowledge of things in general does not enable him to comprehend. I have frequently asked this class of Chinese about matters with which I was already well acquainted, having obtained all the information regarding them from other Chinese, and have always had occasion to be amused by the false notions, or want of all notion, their answers were calculated to give.

I now proceed to particularize some of the false notions alluded to. The following is an instance of one, the more striking as having been entertained only very lately, and perhaps still, by a body of men who are doubtless both intelligent and generally well informed. The East-India Association of Glasgow, in their memorial to Sir Robert Peel, respecting the high English import duties on tea, state :

" 8th. The duty charged by our tariff on tea is equal to 200 per cent. on the shipping cost, viz., 2s. 1d. per lb. on an article which, at an average, costs on board about 1s. ; and while a tariff is negotiating in China for the admission of our productions, it is but reasonable to expect that the Chinese will keep in view the monstrous duty charged in England on their staple."

Now this forms no argument, simply because at the negotiation of the tariff probably not one of the mandarins knew there was any duty on tea at all in England ; and if any of them did know, they would certainly never reflect on the consequences of this duty on their own import trade—caring, as they in fact do, not a straw about any trade whatsoever. I, at all events, know certainly that a mandarin, who had been

constantly employed in the negotiations with
foreigners from their commencement, did not,
after the American treaty was concluded, know
of this English import-duty. When I happened
to mention to him, that a reduction was then
being proposed in England, and that the duty
then existing was double the price of teas in
Canton, he made me repeat what I had said, in
order to make sure that he heard rightly; and
then, instead of making any reflections on its
effect on the trade of his country, he merely
smiled. I am convinced he was admiring the
bold and open way in which the English mandarins levied money from their people, yet somewhat confounded at it; for the whole expression
of his face seemed to say, " You don't do things
by halves; but this is rather strong." Now if it
be borne in mind that this mandarin knew, probably, as much of foreigners as any man of his
class; farther, that his whole chance of rising
depended on the good result of the treaties;
while, on the other hand, if any thing went
wrong his life was in danger; consequently, that
he had every reason to make himself acquainted
with the state of foreign countries; it will be at
once plain how little the Chinese diplomatists
know and think of the principles on which commercial treaties are concluded in the West. Those
engaged in the regulation of the new order of

things had doubtless the wish to show to the
Emperor a large increase in the revenue; but
their object was to quiet the barbarians, whose
wild tempers and unaccountable whims might
easily give rise to fresh disturbances, bringing
certain disgrace, if not death, on those who have
the duty of managing them.

I may state here, that the describing of public
acts, such as the negotiating, signing, and exchanging of treaties, &c., in the same diplomatic
language used in talking of the intercourse between the civilized powers of the West, tends,
however appropriate such language may at bottom be, to give a very false idea of the light in
which the Chinese view these matters; *they* look
on them much as the ministers of the Grecian
empire did their forced dealings with the northern
barbarians.

A great many both contradictory and erroneous
opinions prevail with regard to the population of
China. This the questions frequently asked, as
well as passages in books, such, for instance, as
the following, sufficiently prove. Smith, in his
" Wealth of Nations," says : " The demand for
men, like that for any other commodity, necessarily regulates the production of men ; quickens
it when it goes on too slowly, and stops it when
it advances too fast. It is this demand which
regulates and determines the state of population

in all the different countries of the world—in North America, in Europe, and in China; which renders it rapidly progressive in the first, slow and gradual in the second, and altogether stationary in the last." And this passage is quoted by M'Culloch, in support of the views he maintains with regard to "population" in his "Principles of Political Economy." But we have many good reasons for believing that the state of population in China, far from being stationary in Smith's time, is not so even now, though seventy years of almost uninterrupted peace have elapsed since he wrote. It would seem that people now, when they hear of a country containing 360 millions of inhabitants, the population generally attributed to China, *fancy*, somehow, that this immense collection of human beings is crammed into a territory not greater than that of France or Austria, and that consequently the density of the population must be quite excessive. But the truth is, that China proper, containing, as is well *known*, about 1,300,000 square miles, would have, with its 360 millions of inhabitants, only 277 souls to the square mile, and thus be somewhat less densely populated than England; which latter country has, according to the census of 1841, about 297 souls to the square mile. Now, over all China, husbandry is carried to considerable perfection; over a great part of it two crops of

rice may be had annually; the body of its people
are industrious and economical; but at the same
time all, even those who can barely afford to
feed a wife, marry young, all being exceedingly
anxious to have children; such being the case,
why should its population remain stationary at a
less degree of density than that of England?
We may safely infer, from the results of the last
census, that the population of England has increased since it was taken at the rate of one per
cent. per annum at least, starting from a density
of 297 souls to the square mile ; and the reader
will avoid falling into many erroneous notions,
with regard to China, by viewing that country,
whenever reflecting on subjects influenced by
population, as *twenty-five Englands* placed together.

In books we constantly see the mandarins described as magistrates of *cities* of the 1st, 2nd,
and 3rd ranks ; while the fact of their ruling over
the country towns, villages, and open country surrounding these cities, is left so completely out of
view, that it tends to create a false notion in the
minds of those who do not reflect much on the
subject, and puzzles those who do, by leaving
them in doubt as to who rules over the country.

The improper use of European titles for the
designation of the mandarins is another circumstance which at once proves the existence of, and

tends to propagate, false notions. Thus we, for
instance, frequently see the prefect of Kwang
chôu, or Kwang chôu fu, mentioned as the " Lord
Mayor of Canton "!!* The prefect of Kwang
chôu is the chief local authority of a territory
equalling in extent the kingdom of Holland, and
containing a much larger population. His yaman
is the first court of appeal from fourteen others,
each resembling in their powers our courts of
assize. He is generally a man of some literary
attainments, who has been trained up from his
youth for the civil service, and when he attains
his post, one of a most methodically graduated
series, is the servant of a despotic sovereign, at
whose pleasure he can be removed to the most
distant part of the empire, degraded, dismissed,
or promoted. I need not point out the absurdity
of giving such an officer the title of a Lord Mayor,
the chief magistrate of a city, beyond the walls of
which his comparatively limited authority does
not reach, and whose post, quite republican in its
nature and the manner of its attainment, is generally held for one year only, by a man who spends
all the rest of his life as a merchant.

---

* In the European titles used in these Notes I have generally followed the Chinese Repository. They seem to be the
least inappropriate that could be adopted; but it would, perhaps, be better to employ the Chinese titles, which are short,
and do not mislead.

The Chinese dress—to descend to minor topics —is generally supposed to be quite unchangeable, and the Chinese tailors a kind of stereotype clothiers. Now it is true that the Chinese (I speak of the middle and higher classes) always wear long gowns when they go out, just as we wear coats ; but as every part of our coats and our other garments are constantly being subjected to all kinds of changes, within certain limits, so the length of the Chinese gown, the size and form of its sleeves, its colour, and the kind of flowers worked in it when of silk, &c. &c. are perpetually varying. The same is the case with the Chinese shoes and winter scull-caps : the former are, within certain limits, at one period thick and at another thin-soled ; and the latter are at one time shallow and at another deep, while the silk knob on the top is sometimes small, at others large, &c. &c. In China, in short, we find as many fops as in Europe, who, like their brethren of the West, are so thoroughly versed in matters of dress, that they can at a glance tell you whether a man's clothes be of the latest fashion or not.

The Chinese who speak no English seem to be all quite ignorant of the idea that the eyes painted on the junks are given the latter on account of some (improbable) notion regarding its seeing— an idea that prevails in England in consequence of the old story about " suppose no got eye, how

can see walkee ?" All the junks I have seen with
eyes had also noses and mouths with large tusks
painted on them ; and the Chinese say, that the
object in thus giving the heads of the vessels the
appearance of belonging to a large animal, is to
frighten away the large fish and sea-demons.
This may at first sight seem a very trivial subject
to notice, but as the error prevalent in Europe
regarding it tends, in some degree, to give a false
notion of the Chinese mind, it will hardly be considered trivial by those who would wish to see
the largest nation in the world properly understood.

Errors of a philological nature are, as might be
expected, very numerous. Thus—to refer again
to one of the valuable works of a deservedly distinguished and practical writer—at page 843 of
McCulloch's " Commercial Dictionary " (edition
of 1844) we find it stated that " Nanking is a
European corruption of Kyang ning, the capital
of the extensive province of Kyang nan." Now
Nanking, or, according to the court pronunciation, Nan chîng, is not a corruption, but is the
Chinese name of the old metropolis of the empire,
and means " *southern capital,*" just as Pe king (in
the court pronunciation Pêi chîng) means *northern
capital.* But as two capitals would imply two
sovereigns, the mandarins, regarding Nan-king as
—what it now really is—the chief city of the

province of Chiang nan, and of the department of Chiang nîng, use this latter name in speaking of it. In talking of the present capital they only use the word Chîng, *the capital*, suppressing the word pêi, *northern*, as the use of it would imply the existence of another capital. In this the mandarins follow the works published under the superintendence of the Emperor; but the non-official Chinese of the south frequently use the terms Nan king and Pe king.

As much misconception exists regarding the rendering of European names into Chinese, I would inform the reader, that after being given in the very best manner the Chinese language permits, they are *usually* not recognisable, so deficient is the language in sounds. The Chinese, too, know of course nothing of the derivation of our names, and most of them believe us so wild as to have no surnames; yet I have, on several occasions, seen persons who were gifted with an aristocratic name of baptism before a rather plebeian surname, evince considerable anxiety to have the former given in Chinese, altogether unconscious that John Stubbs sounds to a Chinese ear to the full as noble, and certainly less uncouth, than Montagu Gerald de Beverley would.

These are a few of the false notions afloat regarding China; others are mentioned in the following notes; and I may add, that the number and the nature of the questions asked by gentlemen of good education, and otherwise well informed, have proved to me that the public has much to learn, and not a little to unlearn, respecting the Chinese; and that, therefore, if this publication should be deemed superfluous, it must be solely owing to a faulty execution.

NOTE II.

ON THE BUSINESS STYLE OF THE CHINESE WRITTEN LANGUAGE.

M. REMUSAT, in his "Grammaire Chinoise," notices three styles of the Chinese language, which he calls, *style antique*, *style littéraire*, and *langue des magistrats*, or *langue mandarinique* ; but he is not quite correct in his definitions of these, and he altogether overlooks what I call the *business style* of the Chinese written language, classing the works and documents in which it is found, partly with those which form specimens of the *style antique*, and partly with those in which something like the *langue mandarinique*, or spoken language, is found. He is right when he characterizes the "style antique," or koù wên, as "sententieux, vague, concis, et morcelé," and when he mentions as specimens of it, "des anciens livres classiques appelés *kíng*, des livres de Confucius et des philosophes de son école ;" but wrong when he adds, "ainsi que des écrits relatifs à la politique ou à l'administration, lesquels sont composés même à présent, dans un style imité du koù wên (style antique)," for works on these subjects

are all written in the business style. Further on
he has the following passage, which would lead
one to suppose that the proclamations of the mandarins are written in a style similar to that of the
spoken language, though they are also written in
the business style: "......les écrits qu'on a cou-
tume de composer dans un style analogue à celui
de la langue parlée, tels que les instructions et
les proclamations addressées au peuple......"

That which I call *business style* deserves to be
particularized as such, because a very distinct and
easily definable line of demarcation may be drawn
between it and the other styles of the Chinese
language, and because, as will be shewn below, it
is for, by far, the greater number of foreigners
the most useful to know. The ancient style is
so sententious and concise as to become vague, so
that several of the best specimens of it, as, for
instance, " The Four Books," cannot be understood by the Chinese themselves without an explanation, either written or verbal, *to each new
passage.* It contains, too, a great number of those
characters denominated hsŭ, *empty*, by the Chinese, the influence of which in sentences it is
extremely difficult for Europeans to discern. Now
the business style, though sharing in the peculiar
conciseness of the Chinese language, as compared
with those of Europe, has always so much diffu-
siveness, that any man who has made such pro-

gress as enables him to read one or two works in
that style, will find no difficulty in reading an
entirely new work composed in it. He may occasionally have to apply to his dictionaries for the
meaning of a new term, but the style will no
longer be a difficulty. There is generally nothing
superfluous in it; it is terse, but it is not so concise as to be vague. In the business style the hsŭ,
or empty characters, noticed above, are scarcely
ever used ; in which particular it differs, not only
from the ancient style, but also from the *style littéraire* or wân ch'ang—a term that the Chinese
apply almost exclusively to the compositions of
the candidates at examinations, and others of a
similar nature. The business style differs from
the wân ch'ang in another material point. In
the latter, an appropriate and well understood
term, which does not suit the rhythmus, is ex-
changed for one less suitable in sense and not so
well defined, but which sounds better ; in the
business style, on the other hand, little or no
attention is paid to the rhythmus or sound, but
distinctness being the chief object in view, a word
or term is repeated again and again, whenever its
omission·would appear likely to cause ambiguity.
From the spoken language the business style, like
every other written style, differs very widely. As
a vast number of the Chinese words which are
written quite differently are pronounced exactly

alike, they are obliged in speaking to join others
to them, in order to be understood; just as if we
were obliged, in *speaking* English, to say: sky-
sun, child-son; sacred-holy, all-wholly; only-
sole, spirit-soul; ocean-sea, look-see, &c. &c.;
although there is no mistaking the words sun and
son, holy and wholly, soul and sole, sea and see,
&c. when *written*.   Now in speaking English it
is really not necessary, because our homophonous
words are so few, that the context always leads
the mind of the hearer to the particular word
meant.   Nearly the whole of the Chinese spoken
language is, however, composed of double words,
or compounds (formed in a manner similar to the
above, or in some other manner, but always with
the same object); and these are either not used
at all in writing, or only one of their constituent
parts is used.   The above, and some other differ-
ences, reach to such an extent, that the Chinese
colloquial, or spoken language, and the business
style are, so far as the task of acquiring them is
concerned, really two different languages.   When
we learn French, in learning to speak it we at
the same time learn to read it; but learning the
best spoken Chinese and learning to read the
written language, is like learning to speak the
Parisian French and learning to read Latin. *This
is one cause of the great difficulty of learning the
Chinese;* for the man who has completely mas-

tered the spoken language, and can read the same language when written, is *literally* as far from being able to read a book composed in the comparatively simple business style, as a man who can speak French on all subjects fluently, and read what he speaks when written, is from being able to read the simplest Latin book ; in other words, he is unable to read a single paragraph of it.

The business style is that used in statistical works, in the Ta chîng ghwûi tiên (the collected statutes of the empire), and in the Penal and other codes. It is also used in the addresses of high mandarins and the Boards at Pekin to the Emperor, and in the edicts and rescripts of the latter (hence the Pekin Gazette is entirely written in this style); further, in all the proclamations and notifications of the mandarins ; in their official correspondence with each other ; in petitions from the people to the mandarins, and the answers of the latter ; in judicial decisions, bailbonds, warrants, permits, passports, &c. &c. ; in leases, and deeds of transfer of landed property between private parties ; and in all mercantile-legal papers, as contracts for the performance of work, or for the purchase of goods, promissory notes, and bills of exchange.

In some of the old statutes contained in the Ta chîng ghwûi tiên, and that old part of the Penal Code to which Sir George Staunton chiefly confined himself in his Translation, the business style is very terse, resembling, in so far, the ancient style; but there it distinguishes itself from the latter, by a total want of the empty particles, of which it contains a few in other specimens. It is necessary to remark, however, that there are some histories composed in a style apparently a mixture of the ancient and the business style; and that there are many works which it would be difficult to assign to any one style.

There is still another style which deserves to be noticed, and which, for the sake of distinction, I shall call the *familiar style*. It lies between the business style and the colloquial, and is that in which light works, such as novels, plays, &c. are composed; for it must be observed, even the Chinese plays and the dialogues in novels do not form strictly correct examples of the actually spoken language. The reason is, that much of what is used in the spoken language is not only unnecessary to express the same idea on paper, but would, as useless verbiage, rather cause obscurity; just as it would render the English obscure if we were to write sky-sun, child-son, &c. when the words sun and son are of themselves sufficiently distinct. The style in plays is, however, a near approach to the actual spoken language, and even the narrative in novels contains a great admixture of it.

To recapitulate : the *ancient style* is sententious, so concise as to be vague and unintelligible
without explanations ; contains a great number of
the difficult *hsŭ* or empty particles, but does not
confine itself by a strict attention to the rhythmus. The best specimens of it are to be found
in the ancient classics, the works of Confucius,
and of the philosophers of the same school. The
Chinese say of this style, that it is *very profound.*

The *wán ch'ang,* or *literary style,* is sufficiently
diffuse to be intelligible, contains a great number
of the empty particles, and conforms strictly to
the rhythmus. The compositions of the literary
graduates at the examinations are almost the only
specimens of this style, all compositions in which
are characterized by a constant reference to a
theme or text. The Chinese say of this style,
that it is *very abstract.*

The *business style* is always sufficiently diffuse
to be intelligible ; it always contains few, many
specimens of it none, of the empty particles ; and
it does not confine itself by any attention to the
rhythmus. Works on government and statistics,
and the laws, are comprised in this style ; and all
documents of a legal nature, all official correspondence and private correspondence on business,
are written in it. The Chinese say of this style,
that it is *plain and distinct.*

The *familiar style* is the least terse of any of
c 2

the Chinese written styles; it contains very few of the empty particles, it does not confine itself by any attention to the rhythmus, and contains a considerable admixture of terms used in the spoken language.

The narrative parts of novels form examples of this style, which the Chinese designate as *plain but shallow.*

The *colloquial Chinese** is the least terse style in the language; it contains no characters that can fairly be classed with those called empty, and in it, of course, not the slightest attention is paid to the rhythmus.

Plays and the dialogues in novels are written in a style nearly resembling the colloquial Chinese, and sentences precisely the same as those used in oral conversation occur not unfrequently in such writings; but I have never seen any continuous piece in the exact spoken language.

The above enables us to form an opinion as to the proper style to study. Missionaries may, possibly, find it useful to study the ancient style, in order to acquaint themselves with Chinese ethics in the original language. But every moment that the government servant or the merchant spends in the study of the ancient style, is altogether misemployed. I mention this because

* I refer here to the general oral language of the country, as spoken by the mandarins, not to any of the dialects.

it is very much the custom in Europe to commence the study of the language with the classi-
cal " Four Books," a work that is entirely written
in the ancient style. Now a man may, doubtless,
with the assistance of a translation and explanations, go through the whole of the " Four Books,"
and render himself, in a great measure, master of
the original. But this would be a task to him
who commenced with that classic of at least a
couple of years of unremitting study; and when
he had finished it, he would be totally unable to
make a correct translation of the simplest official
letter or mercantile contract. A thorough knowledge of the " Four Books " in the original is, too,
as useless to the man who wishes to translate business papers from English into Chinese, as it is to
him who wishes to translate similar papers from
Chinese into English; for, even supposing him
able (a *very* bold supposition) to compose in the
style of that work, the want of business terms
would offer an insuperable difficulty; and if he
were to finish his task by borrowing these from a
dictionary, the Chinese would probably not understand what he had written, so concise and vague
is the ancient style. In short, for the British
officer or merchant to study the " Four Books,"
with a view of making a practical use of what he
learns, is rather more absurd than it would be for
the mandarin or the Chinese merchant to study

Proverbs and Ecclesiastes, with the view of writing to, and drawing up their agreements with the English in the style of these books.*

The first business of the foreign government agent or merchant, who intends studying the Chinese, is to learn to speak, which can be best done by reading some work in the *familiar style*, as a play or novel, with a good teacher, paying, however, still more attention to the language the latter uses in conversation, than to that contained in the books. When the student is able to converse with some degree of ease, and can understand the explanations of his teacher, he should commence reading the more easy compositions in the business style, as the proclamations of local mandarins, contracts, &c. ; and, as he gradually progresses in his knowledge of the language, proceed to read the Pekin Gazette, and the various books which are enumerated above as being written in the business style.

When, in the following Notes, the Chinese written language is spoken of, it must be understood that the business style is chiefly alluded to.

* Those foreigners, however, who have the leisure, and wish to understand the people thoroughly, would do well to read translations of the " Four Books," and the other Chinese classics.

NOTE III.

ON THE DIFFICULTY OF LEARNING THE CHINESE LANGUAGE.

ONE cause of the difficulty of learning to speak and read the Chinese language has been pointed out in the preceding Note, viz., the spoken differs so much from the written style, that those who learn the Chinese, learn, in reality, two languages. This, with some other difficulties—as, the very peculiar construction ; the great want of grammatical particles, which in other languages serve to show the gender and number of nouns, the tenses of verbs, &c. ; and even the want in the written language of all punctuation, or of a visible division into separate paragraphs—are inseparable from the language, and will always make it the most difficult to acquire of those now existing.

But at present the student has to encounter another difficulty, not arising from any peculiarity of the language, and which is by far the greatest ; this is, *the want of a good dictionary.*

Morrison's Dictionary (the one I have found most useful) does him, as it would any one man, great honour. It is impossible to use it without feeling respect for the talent and industry of the author, and the student even learns to look back with a kind of gratitude to the man who has done so much to lighten his labours. Nevertheless, it must be confessed that Morrison's Dictionary not only has many faults, but that it is *very* defective, when compared, in point of perfectness, with the best French-English, French-German, or German-English dictionaries. This is a truth that continually forces itself on the notice of the student, and becomes plainer to him as his knowledge of the language increases. What the French sinologue, M. Julien, says of Chinese poetry is equally true of the business style. " La poesie chinoise abonde de mots polysyllabes, qui ne se trouvent point dans nos dictionnaires, et dont les parties composantes, traduit littéralement, ne sauraient donner le sens.........Dans ce travail, tout nouveau pour moi, j'ai été vingt fois arrêté, soit par des expressions figurées, soit par des mots composés, dont l'analyse ne saurait donner le sens, et qui ne se trouvent ni dans les vocabulaires publiés par les Européens, ni dans les dictionnaires tout chinois que j'ai à ma disposition."*

Scarcely one proclamation is issued that does not contain several words, generally compounds, which are not contained in Morrison's Dictionary, and the same is the case with nearly every leaf

* L'Histoire du Cercle du Craie, préface.

of the Chinese Codes. Hence the student who makes any considerable progress in the Chinese language is obliged to *compose a dictionary;* and when the reader reflects what an extent of varied and solid knowledge, how much sound judgment, as well as fertility of imagination, and what untiring industry a man must possess to perform such a task, even with a moderate degree of success, he will not wonder at the paucity of Chinese scholars of any note. If the student of Chinese do not possess, in some degree, the acquirements and talents that fit a man to become a lexicographer, he stops in his progress at a certain point ; he cannot proceed beyond the narrow limits prescribed by the deficiencies of the dictionaries, and though he employs a life-time in working at the Chinese, his translations, whether from Chinese into English, or from English into Chinese, are, to the last, unidiomatic and incorrect.

The greatest obstacle, then, in the way of those who would learn the Chinese language is the want of a good dictionary. In learning German or French (and I suppose any other European language) the memory is almost the only faculty that is called into play; the completeness of the dictionaries prevents the necessity of exerting any other of the mental capacities. But in learning Chinese, memory, judgment, imagination, and patience are all tried ; and according as the student

possesses these qualities in greater or less perfection, and as he possesses or is wanting in a good
knowledge of his own language, so his progress
will be quick or slow.

The lexicographers, hitherto, have not done
much more than translate the meanings given in
Kanghsi's Chinese Dictionary, a sort of Chinese
Johnson, so far as its great use in the country is
concerned, but which was compiled by a number
of different persons, by the order of the Kanghsi
emperor. But if we exclude the merely scientific
terms, and regard many of the less important
variations of a word as making but one with itself,
the English language contains, at a moderate estimation, about 20,000 words. Of these few, even
among reading people, have more than five or six
thousand at their command. Now the lexicographers, in translating Kanghsi's Dictionary, seem
to have only employed such English words as
were at their command, and have thus made Chinese-English dictionaries containing not one-third
part of the existing English words in general use.
This accounts for the total want of an English-
Chinese dictionary; for when these lexicographers
would compose one by reversing their Chinese-
English dictionaries, they are at once stopped
short by the want of English words. We have
indeed got two vocabularies; one by Dr. Morrison, forming the third part of his dictionary, and

the other by Mr. Williams. But these contain
only a very small proportion of the English words
in common use ; hence, as the reader who is accustomed to translate from English into a foreign
language will at once perceive, it is excessively
difficult to translate from English into Chinese,
since, in order to do it with some degree of ease,
it is necessary for the translator to have an extensive collection of synonymous words and phrases
in his memory, which in other languages are supplied by the dictionaries.

It is evidently not in the power of any one, or
even of two or three individuals, however talented
and industrious they may be, to compile a complete dictionary of two copious, but in every other
respect very dissimilar, languages ; and it is certain that we shall not have a good Chinese-English, much less an English-Chinese dictionary,
until we have before us the contributions of a
great many sinologues, who have laboured independently, and have ascertained the meanings of
the words by a careful collation of different passages in which they occur, availing themselves, at
the same time, of all the assistance native or the
already existing foreign dictionaries may afford.
Such sinologues must, too, have confined their
attention each chiefly to one of the styles, without which they will not be able to make additions to be depended on.

In the existing Chinese-English dictionaries, sometimes the particular meaning of the word which it has in the passage to be translated is altogether wanting. At other times that sense of the word is not altogether unnoticed, but instead of the synonymous English term, we find only a translation of its Chinese definition, as the latter stands in the native dictionaries, forming a very vague indication of the exact meaning of the word. It is, however, the words composed of two characters, and compounds generally, that occasion the most trouble ; for as they are seldom contained in Kanghsi's Dictionary (of which, as above stated, the foreign dictionaries are little more than translations), great numbers of them are not given at all in these latter. The meanings which each of the characters have when standing alone, may indeed be given, but, in many instances, such meanings form no clue to their signification when standing together as a compound. To increase the difficulty, the Chinese characters are, when forming compounds, not joined together as in European languages, but stand just as they do when used singly, so that the translator must in each case himself determine, from the context, whether they form a compound or not ; just as if the English word *manhood* was, when signifying virility or manly qualities, written *man hood*, in which case a foreigner

might think a head-dress of some kind was meant.
Let us suppose a Frenchman learning the English language with one of the first compiled Eng-
lish-French dictionaries; suppose this dictionary
to contain the word *court* and all its various meanings, also the word *ship* and its meaning when
standing alone, but neither the word *courtship*,
nor any description of the influence of the particle
ship in compounds, and we have a case parallel to
many that occur in studying the Chinese. Let
us suppose the Frenchman to meet with the following sentence in an English book : " While the
courtship was going on." " Courtship, ship of the
court? royal yacht? vessel of war?" he would
ask himself. " Or does it mean some kind of vessel with a deck resembling a court-yard? But
where can it have been going to? And why is it
mentioned here?" Then, seeing perhaps farther
on mention made of a marriage, he would run on
making surmises in a different track. " Um—
courtship—perhaps there is some kind of ship in
the courts of law, that when marriages—but no,
that would be a very extraordinary custom. Court
means to flatter—flatter ship.—Can it be that the
English send wedding presents in a vessel made
like a ship?" Suddenly a bright idea flashes on
his mind. " By the by! They call their ships
she, why should they not call their shes ships?
They are a maritime nation, very fond of their

ships, and, it is to be hoped, fond of their women
too.   Court she—flatter she.—While the a-flat-
tering she was going on.   Precisely the thing!"
And thus, though by a false track, he might be
led to the true meaning of the word.   Let the
reader not be surprised at this outbreak in the
midst of a grave discourse on such a dry topic as
dictionary-making.   In trying to arrive at the
true meaning of words not contained in the dictionaries, the imagination, as above stated, must
be kept constantly in play.   It will, indeed, occasionally enable the translator to jump at the real
signification of a term at once, but even in this
case corroboration is necessary; and, in the great
number of instances, the true meanings of the
words can only be ascertained by a diligent and
unprejudiced collation of a number of different
passages in which it is contained—passages that
cannot be collected and compared without much
manual, and still more mental labour.

As this is a subject which will well bear en-
larging on, I subjoin a few remarks having reference to the Chinese language in particular, followed by some examples in illustration.   They
will, it is hoped, be of some use to the beginner,
and at the same time prove the correctness of the
preceding statements concerning the imperfections
of the existing dictionaries.

When a word or words occur in a passage, the

meanings of which, as given in the dictionaries, do not make any sense at all in connection with the other words of the passage, or, though communicating an idea to the mind, sound odd to the English ear, the translator must of course find out and adopt some new meanings, giving the exact sense of the original in idiomatic English. Or when, as often happens, the dictionaries give to words occurring in a passage a great number of meanings nearly similar, yet with perceptible shades of difference among them, and sometimes even differing widely, but all of which would, if adopted, make sense with the other words of the passage, the translator has to fix on such as seem best, i. e. most correct.

In all these cases the grand rule is, to find out and make a list of a number of different passages in which the word the signification of which is to be ascertained occurs ; and then to adopt for it such a meaning as is found on trial to suit perfectly, both in sense and sound, in each of the different passages, and to be consonant to the general nature of the subjects discussed. There is another rule which will often be found of considerable assistance. That is, adopt such a word in the English language as, both in its original or physical, and in its figurative or moral meanings, is used in the same manner as the Chinese word the signification of which is to be fixed ; or, if

the words are not used in a physical sense, adopt
such as have derived their synonymous figurative,
or secondary, meanings in the same manner from
the original, or primary, signification. It must
be remembered, however, that this last rule is
merely auxiliary to the first, independently of
which it cannot be safely applied; for many words
and terms which are synonymous in their physical
senses are no longer so when used figuratively.

Take, for example, the very simple Chinese
compound, 不 願 *pu yuên*. According to Morrison, *pu* means *not*, and the following is his explanation of yuên: " From *origin*, or *source*, and
head. A large head ; to stretch out the head, as
in looking for with expectation. The direction
of the heart to an object, to desire, to wish, that
to which the heart is directed, an object of desire.
Each; every; a short appearance of the face.
A vow." Now you perceive, from the nature of
the subject, that *not to wish, not to desire*, is the
meaning of the compound in the sentence before
you, but both of these expressions sound oddly in
it. You then remember—a fact which is, however, not mentioned in the dictionaries, but must
be found out by experience—that the Chinese *pu*
must often be rendered by the English negative
particle *un*, and you think of *unwilling*, but this
also sounds oddly. You then recollect the rule,
that many Chinese negatives must be translated

by an affirmative of an opposite meaning, and repugnant, averse, reluctant, &c. occur to you; when, by having recourse to the original and physical meanings of the terms, you perceive that as yuên means, *to stretch out the head as in looking for with expectation*, and *to wish for*, therefore *pu yuên*, from the power of the Chinese negative, may mean, *to turn away the head from disinclination*, and hence that *averse*, the physical or literal sense of which is, *to turn away from, in manifestation of dislike*, must be the synonymous word in English; an opinion in which you are fully confirmed by trying it in four or five different passages in which *pu yuên* occurs.

As a second example, we may take the compound 頂 撞 *ting chwang*. It is not contained in the dictionaries, but the following are Morrison's explanations of its component parts, *ting* and *chwang*.

Ting. "From *nail* and *head*. The summit; the vertex; the top of a hill; to carry on the top of the head; the thing carried; the knob of different colours worn on the top of the cap by the Tartar Chinese, to distinguish rank." Then follow some compounds, all of which refer only to the knob worn by the mandarins on the cap.

Chwang. "To grasp with the hand and pound. To beat; to strike suddenly; abrupt; to rush

D

against; to bounce upon; to knock; to take or seize."

Now, in all the phrases you have collected containing the compound *ting chwang*, it is impossible to make any use of the meanings given to *ting;* and if you are only commencing the language, this character brings you to a stand-still. If you have, however, attained some proficiency in speaking, you may have learnt, from your own experience, that this word means *to oppose,* or *against,* as in *ting fûng, against the wind; ting shwûi, against the water;* and hence conclude that the words *ting chwang* might mean, *to oppose and beat,* or *to beat against.* But from the nature of the subjects in your examples, and in particular from the circumstance of *ting chwang* being frequently preceded by the words *chu yên, to put forth words,* you perceive that the compound *ting chwang* must be taken in a moral, not a physical sense; and that it must have the meaning of *contend, argue, debate, altercate,* or *dispute.* By referring, then, to the original physical meaning of these words, you soon find that *debate* and *dispute,* derived from words signifying *to strike, drive,* or *beat,* are the most suitable. The Chinese expression is, however, always used of the language of inferiors to superiors, or at all events to equals, never of the language of superiors to inferiors; a circumstance that agrees well with the primary meaning of *ting.*

This seems, from the component parts of the character, to have been *the point or top of the head* (hence TING *chwang, to beat* or *bounce* UPWARDS), and has probably obtained its use in the sense of *opposition to*, or *contention*, from the circumstance of sheep, goats, oxen, and other animals butting with the head when they fight. And, indeed, when you ask a Chinese, how these animals fight? he usually answers by, *tôu tïng tôu, head ting head*, i. e. *head against* or *opposing* head. This meaning of *ting* is not given in any of the dictionaries.

Every individual language contains words which have no one synonym in any other; and, as might be expected from the long isolation of the Chinese, their language contains a large proportion of them. The word 據 *chŭ*, which occurs often in official papers, is an instance of one. Its meaning is, *to hold* or *have in possession as proof, or as a ground for action;* but frequently the idea of *having in possession* predominates so much, while those of *proof* or *ground for action* are so subordinate, that the word can only be rendered, correctly and idiomatically, by *receive.* It is then like *have* in the mercantile phrase, "We have yours of such and such a date." At other times, the idea of *having in possession* is so completely sunk, and one of the others so predominant, that the word must be rendered either by *grounding on, according to,* or *in consequence of.* The dictionaries are generally very defective in their explanations of this kind of words.

As a striking instance of the manner in which the imperfections of the dictionaries are the cause of odd sounding translations, I may instance the word 明 *ming*. The meanings of this word given in the dictionaries are, *clear, bright, perspicuous,* and others of a similar signification ; and every one who has been in the habit of reading the soi-disant translations alluded to, must have remarked the frequent and displeasing recurrence of the word *clearly*. According to these translations, every thing must be, ought to be, has been, or has not been, done clearly. The reason is, that the dictionaries do not even hint at the material fact, that *ming* is often only an auxiliary particle, denoting the successful completion of the action expressed by the verb with which it is in connection. In many cases it is, therefore, fully translated by placing such verb in the perfect, or the second future, tense, but often an entirely new word must be substituted. Thus 查 *cha*, means, *to make an examination,* but *cha ming* does not mean, *to make a clear examination ;* it means, to ascertain : 議 *i*, means, *to consult,* but *i ming* does not mean, *to consult clearly ;* it means, to agree on : still less does 言 *yên, to talk,* mean with *ming, to talk clearly ;* it is sometimes used, with this affix, in the sense of, *to state distinctly,* but more com-

monly, it then means, *to stipulate or agree on.* The
Chinese terms, in this last example, are exactly
like the German reben and abreben, the *ming* having
the same power as the particle ab.

What has been said above will, in some measure, account to the reader for the many odd
things that are given to the public as translations
from the Chinese; proving, as it must, to him,
that it requires several years of constant study of
one style of the Chinese written language, to enable a man to make a tolerable translation of a
document written in that style. It is always an
invidious and thankless task to find fault, and the
soi-disant translations alluded to are probably
welcome to many people, in the absence of better
renderings; but when they—though abounding
with gross errors, and containing internal evidence
that the translators did not understand the original sufficiently to distinguish where one sentence
ended and another began—are trumpeted as the
work of "critical masters of the Chinese language," "the first Chinese scholars of the age,"
&c., a word of warning becomes necessary, to prevent the public from forming a very false notion
of Chinese composition. A perfect translation
ought to give the exact sense of the original, in a
style closely resembling that of the latter; that

is to say, if the style of the original is fine and easy, the style of the translation ought also to be fine and easy; if formal and stiff, the style of the translation must also be formal and stiff; and when the style of the original is obscure, the style of the translation should also be obscure. Now, by keeping this definition in view, even the reader whose philological attainments do not extend beyond the knowledge of his own language, can easily perceive of himself, that the great majority of things published as translations from the Chinese (I refer chiefly to those intended to be translations of official documents) do not deserve the name, and that they are, in fact, wretched. They are not English, even if we consider them sentence by sentence, and each sentence by itself. If we consider them as a whole, we observe a total want of all logical relation between the sentences. There seems to be no reasoning, no continuous train of thought in them ; they are merely a succession of abrupt exclamations, invectives, opinions, and mandates, having little or no connection with each other. But the Chinese have been a literary people and great writers for upwards of 2,000 years; there is probably more written on practical business in China than in Great Britain, for a vast amount of legislative and legal business, which in the latter country is got through orally, is here transacted on paper; the Chinese are

generally considered a sober-minded, rational people; and, indeed, the man who enters into an
argument with them on subjects they understand,
must have all his wits about him, without which,
and without reason on his side, he need not hope
to prevail. Now such being the case, is it not
very extraordinary that they cannot write common sense in their official documents? The fact
is (and it is a truth that must daily become more
apparent to the student, as his knowledge of the
language increases), the Chinese official and legal
documents, especially the former, are, from the
methodical, distinct manner in which they first
state the grounds their arguments are based on,
from the closeness of the reasoning they contain,
the absence of all useless verbiage, and the constant
subservience of sound to sense, generally superior
to English documents of the same nature. The
reason of this superiority seems to be, that the
Chinese official documents are prepared by the
shï ye—men who have spent a large portion of
their lives at that work—and must be sanctioned
by the mandarins, themselves generally men of
talent and high literary attainments. The reader,
in forming an opinion of Chinese writing, must
not be led astray by certain formal expressions
that occur at the beginning and end of proclamations and official letters ; and which, even when
best translated, sound somewhat odd. After all,

the Chinese, though apt to use high-flown expressions in private correspondence, have in their official letters nothing so outrageous as, " I have the honour to be, Sir, your most obedient, humble servant," &c. &c. ; and it would be easy to show, that in many other of the minor points their method is really better than ours.

It is worthy of remark, however, that the higher mandarins, in corresponding with the diplomatic agents of western nations, have adopted the custom of these latter of appending some complimentary phrases at the end of their official letters —a thing they never do among themselves.

NOTE IV.

ON THE COLLOQUIAL CHINESE AS SPOKEN BY THE MANCHOOS, INCLUSIVE OF THE IMPERIAL FAMILY AND HOUSEHOLD, AND BY NATIVES OF PEKIN GENERALLY.

THIS is commonly called the " Pekin dialect," but it is, in reality, the standard spoken language of the country, holding the same place in China that the London English, as spoken by the educated classes, maintains in the British isles, and the Parisian French in France. If we find educated and rich Chinese, as, for instance the Hong merchants at Canton, making use of a provincial dialect, differing widely from the Pekin colloquial, we must bear in mind the great extent of the country, the number of its inhabitants, and the difficulty of intercommunication, as compared with the so much smaller states of Europe; and that, after all, it (the Pekin colloquial) is spoken without the slightest variation, either in the collocation of the words or their pronunciation, by a far greater number of individuals than any other language in the world. Even allowing, what indeed would seem to have been the case, that it has

been formed as it now exists by the present reigning family and their Manchoo followers, who had
to learn the Chinese as a foreign language; still
the present dynasty has had quiet possession of
the whole country for about 200 years; the change
made by them in the court language has not been
very great, as a comparison with the plays of
former dynasties will prove; the language used
by the rulers is sure to be imitated; and the
Chinese system of government is peculiarly calculated to insure this. Hence we need not be
surprised that the colloquial Chinese, as spoken
by the Imperial family and the natives of Pekin
generally, is not only in almost universal use
among those in any way connected with government or government offices, but is also in great
use among merchants.

After what I have just said, my readers will
be astonished to learn, that in no work has an
attempt yet been made to give the Pekin pronunciation of the Chinese characters in the Roman alphabet. The elder Morrison, it is true,
was too practical a man* to neglect it altogether,

* When, in any of these Notes, I chance to make depre-
ciating remarks on the works of this gentleman, I would have
it to be distinctly understood, that it is always with the reser-
vation, that I consider he has done far more than any other
person whatever to extend a knowledge of the Chinese language and people among Western nations. It was absolutely
impossible that his philological works should be faultless, or

and the student will accordingly find a note on the subject in the introduction to Part I. of his dictionary ; nevertheless, he has, in all his works, given what is called the Nankin pronunciation, probably following therein the Jesuit missionaries who lived at court during the reign of Kang hsi, about 150 years ago. Later writers have closely adhered to this pronunciation, *however much they may have varied the orthography used to express it ;* and hence it follows, that in no work yet published do we find the true court pronunciation of the colloquial Chinese. The chief reason is, I suppose, that we have, till lately, had no intercourse with mandarins or their people. Now, however, it is, I venture to say, the pronunciation most deserving of the attention of the generality of students.

Of 231 civil mandarins, taken at random from among those stationed in the distant province of Kwang-tûng, in the end of 1844, I find that 74 were natives of Pekin, 15 were natives of different parts of Chĭli, the province in which Pekin

leave nothing to be done by future labourers ;—but the second part of his dictionary still continues to be by far the most useful work on the Chinese language extant ; and throughout his works generally, there is scattered a vast deal of interesting and, particularly, of *practically useful* information. Too much praise cannot be meted to him for his exertions, nor to the East-India Company for the munificent manner in which it supported them.

is situated, and 142 were from other provinces.
I may therefore state it as a fact, that one third
of the civilians, almost the only people with whom
we have any intercourse, speak the Chinese colloquial *only* as is done at Pekin ; while, as far as I
can judge from my own experience, all the others
speak it in the same manner tolerably well, much
better, it may be safely asserted, than in any
other manner, except, perhaps, that which obtains
in their respective native districts.   Of all the
mandarins of different ranks with whom I have
held conversations, during a three years' residence
in Canton, while fully one half spoke the pure
Pekin colloquial, and the language of all ap-
proached it more or less, *not one* used the pronunciation given as the mandarin by Morrison,
and by Mr. Medhurst, in their dictionaries, and
as the court dialect by Mr. Williams (with a different orthography), in his vocabulary.   It may
be, however, that the pronunciation followed by
these gentlemen is, in some measure, used by
civilians, natives of Kwang-tûng, all of whom are,
in accordance with Chinese policy, stationed in
other provinces.

In addition to what I have said above, proving
that the Pekin colloquial is entitled to be considered *the* spoken language of the empire, like the
London English in the British dominions, I may
state, that it is understood, to a considerable ex-

tent, by the lowest classes of Canton and its vicinity, a neighbourhood where such a very distinct
patois is the common language.

A knowledge of it has spread from the yamun,
among the numerous inhabitants of which it is
used in daily intercourse, and thus it has happened that when I have, at Whampoa, met with
a common boatman unable to speak the English
jargon in general use between foreigners and
natives, and have, in my ignorance of the local
patois, tried him with the Pekin, I have found
myself not only understood, but readily answered.

Hence, as it is quite impossible to attain a *practical proficiency* in any two variations of the colloquial, it will certainly be found most advisable
for the greater part of those who intend studying
the language with the view of putting their knowledge to actual use in business, to apply themselves to the Pekin alone, as a spoken medium.
Missionaries, who should preach to the common
people, ought of course to make themselves, each
one, master of one of the dialects spoken by that
class; but the merchant, who might have occasion to reside at different parts, and to converse
with native merchants from different provinces,
will, I think, find the colloquial of the court, on
the whole, the most useful; while the man who
wishes to become a really efficient government

servant in China, should apply himself assiduously
to it, and to it only.

What I have said above, as to the impossibility
of acquiring any practical proficiency in more
than one variety of the colloquial, requires some
explanation. A man endowed with a little per-
severance may attain a good practical knowledge
of three or four European and other *syllabic* languages ; but such is by no means the case with
the Chinese dialects. It is those very peculiar
attributes of the Chinese language, called intonations, or shĕng, the subjects of Note VI., which
form the difficulty, the great stumbling-block in
short, of those who attempt more than one variety of the colloquial ; and I think it will appear,
from that Note, that the obstacle is a serious one.
In addition to that, the vowel and consonantal
sounds, the collocation of the characters, and even
the characters themselves, differ in the various
patois, in the Nankin and in the Pekin colloquial ;
and these difficulties, taken together, are so great,
that even a man possessing a considerable natural
talent for languages, i. e. a good memory, pliable
organs of speech, and a quick ear, will, I reassert,
find it impossible to acquire a useful proficiency
in more than one ; while if, instead of concentrat-
ing his faculties, he disperse them by attempting
to learn two or three, he will doubtless become

able, in time, to give a laboured utterance to certain successions of sounds, that, taken as Chinese,
may occasionally constitute sentences of a dialect,
but which, generally, will form parts of no language whatever ; and he will certainly never be
able to speak any variety of the Chinese colloquial with that degree of readiness which, in these
days of the division of labour, is entitled to be
called practical proficiency.

I must here warn the beginner against supposing, that because a Chinese when you are talking
to him smiles, inclines his head, and says, Ah!
Um! &c. that he therefore understands you.
Though the Chinese may scarcely understand a
single sentence of what is uttered, their national
urbanity will generally induce them to do this for
half an hour together, and they will not, in fact,
let their non-comprehension be perceived, unless
the subject be one they consider important.

The two following Notes, in the first of which
a new orthography, adapted to the Pekin colloquial, is proposed, and the second of which is a
dissertation on the intonations, or shĕng, will, I
trust, be found useful to the student commencing
the Chinese spoken language.

NOTE V.

A NEW ORTHOGRAPHY, ADAPTED TO THE PEKIN
PRONUNCIATION OF THE COLLOQUIAL CHINESE.

IN the preceding Note I have remarked, that in no work yet published has the true court, or Pekin, pronunciation of the colloquial Chinese been given; and as I soon found the already existing orthographies altogether unsuitable to express it, I was obliged to frame a new one. It was intended at first solely for my own use, but I now lay it before the philological public, in the hope that it may prove of some assistance to beginners.

I first proceed to give my reasons for not adhering either to Morrison's orthography, or to that adopted in Dr. Bridgman's " Chinese Chrestomáthy," and in Williams's " English and Chinese Vocabulary," in order to express the Pekin pronunciation.

The latter mentioned system is, in the intrʋduction to the Chrestomathy, said to have been proposed by Sir William Jones, and to have been, with some variations, since very widely adapted in India, the Pacific islands, and North America.

In the Chrestomathy, it has again been varied to suit the Canton dialect, and it might be asked, if any additions were necessary for the court pronunciation, why were they not made, and the system retained in substance? But the question is, should a man who devotes several years of his life to the study of the language of an immense empire, such as that of China, keep using an awkward orthography, or even one not perfectly suitable, merely because it has been used to reduce to writing the languages spoken by the savages in the Pacific islands, and in North America, or those of the semi-barbarous natives of India? I should certainly say not, but that, on the contrary, in the study of such a difficult language as the Chinese, every thing ought to be made as convenient as possible, without reference to any other language whatsoever. This, then, was my reason, when I found several new sounds in the court pronunciation, for framing an entirely new system, having reference to that pronunciation alone; and if I have succeeded in rendering it more simple and distinct than that used in the Chrestomathy, with the necessary additions, would have been, I shall consider myself perfectly justified in having proposed it.

The sounds I call new are such as I have never heard in any language, except in the Chinese as pronounced by natives of Pekin, and which certainly do not exist in either the English, French, or German. In the orthographies hitherto used, such sounds, vowel and consonantal, as could not be exactly expressed by any of the letters of European languages, have been left unexpressed, except by an apostrophe, or some similar mark, used for all. Mr. Williams, in the introduction to his Vocabulary, calls the new sounds noticed by him, " imperfect vowels." He says : " The best mode of writing the collection of sounds here grouped together under the name of *imperfect vowels,* has puzzled writers on the Chinese language not a little. No distinct vowel sound is perceivable in any of them ; and after comparing the attempts that have been made to express the sound that is heard by some vowel, perhaps the best way is to leave it unexpressed, using an apostrophe to denote its place, and writing only the consonants." But an " imperfect vowel " is in reality an impossibility. To prevent a misunderstanding from the attaching of different ideas to the same words, I must remind the reader, that *whenever the human* VOICE *is used, utterance is given to some vowel,* and that *a vowel is always a simple sound,* i. e. *one which may be prolonged without any movement in the organs of speech, as long as respiration permits.* As soon as the organs of speech are moved, the sound is modulated, and the whole becomes thereby a diphthong ; and if their position be changed a second time, the whole enunciation becomes triphthongal. Thus the letters i and u, as heard in thine and cube, are both diphthongs, while the au in plausible, and the ea in plead, are simple vowel sounds; the oi in spoil, the ou in sound, are diphthongs; the a in man, the i in pin, and the e in me, are simple vowels.

Now in those sounds which Mr. Williams calls " imperfect vowels," the Chinese can and do use the *voice* as loudly, and prolong them as much, as in pronouncing any other sounds of the language. They constitute, therefore, according to the above definitions, vowels as perfect as any we use; and to make any distinction between them and other vowels *as such*, merely because they do not occur in our languages, tends, like every distinction without a difference, only to confuse.

For this reason, I have represented all new sounds I have remarked in the Pekin pronunciation, whether vowel or consonantal, by letters of the Roman alphabet, with a half-circle over them; and thus the new vowels, as expressed by ĕ, ĭ, and ŏ, have, to an Englishman, nothing more strange in their appearance than the German ö and ü. The sounds, too, represented by them are not more difficult for an Englishman to acquire than the sounds expressed by these two German letters. The half-circle in the following orthography, invariably indicates a new sound, whereby, as above stated, I understand one with which there is nothing homophonous, either in the English, the German, or the French. The only exception is the ŭ, which represents a very common vowel of the two latter languages.*

The consonantal sound represented by ğ is a very peculiar one. In the orthography used by Mr. Williams, and by Dr. Bridgman in the Chinese Chrestomathy, a consonantal sound (which does not, however, occur in the Pekin pronunciation) is represented by the first ng in singing. That sound somewhat resembles the one represented by ğ, but the nasal part of it must be omitted. An idea of it may be formed, by trying to pronounce the g in gun without pressing the tongue against the roof of the mouth.

One defect of the other orthography noticed above is, that some very different sounds are represented by a coalition of letters and diacritical marks but slightly differing in appearance. I have striven to avoid this, as much as possible, in the orthography now proposed, considering it of importance that the eye should be easily able to catch the difference, whenever one is intended.

* Morrison, in his Dictionary (Part I. Vol. i. xvii., and Part II. Vol. i. 620), and Williams, in his Vocabulary (Introd. viii. 13), err in considering this sound, represented here by ŭ, and the French eu as homophonous ; a circumstance which I mention, as the inconsistencies consequent on this error in the works of the former, confused me not a little, on commencing the Chinese. The French eu has this sound only in the tenses of the auxiliary verb avoir.

It will be remarked, that I have omitted the sz and the tsz which occur in all English orthographies, and are represented by the French as " ss and ts sifflant." The fact is, that although when a Chinese pronounces the words, in which the sounds intended to be expressed by these letters occur, they may at first seem to be merely a peculiar buzz, yet on listening attentively, and particularly when he pronounces them slowly, it will be found that the buzzing consonantal sound ceases at the commencement ; and that it is, in the one case, merely the sound of the sharp English s in sand, and in the other that of the German ʒ in Zahe, or in the English ts in Whitsuntide. *The peculiarity of the sound does not, therefore, lie in the consonant, but in the vowel;* which is, in fact, the one I represent by ĭ.

The English w, in the orthography now proposed, must not be supposed homophonous with the French ou, a coalition which, in French orthographies, occupies its place. The French substitute the ou for the English w, which is a distinct *consonantal* sound, only because the latter does not exist, under any form, in their language.

The German sounds referred to in the following tables, are those heard in the words as pronounced by the educated classes in Hanover, whose pronunciation of the German corresponds well with the orthography of that language.

I. Simple Vowels.

Vowel of New Orthog.	Homophonous Sounds in the English, German, or French Languages.	Examples in Chinese.	
a	a in father ; a in man … …	慢	茶
â	As the last a in American … …	能	燈
e	a in fate ; é in dé, coté … …	也	野
ê	e in met … … … …	言	葉
ĕ	Between the ö in störrig, and the o in Nord. *Resembling* the eu in beurre (much broader than the eû in jeûne or the eu in jeune) …	正	身
i	i in pique, police, and ee in seed ; i in mir … … … … …	喜	衣
î	i in pin, thin … … … …	巾	氷
ĭ	*Resembling* the i in him, chin, &c., but the teeth are nearly closed in the formation of the sound … …	知	子
o	o in no … … … …	過	所
ô	o in not … … … …	着	活
ŏ	*Resembling* the eu in meute, with an approach to the o in nos. Between the o in Lord and the i in him, but most like the former … …	個	色
u	u in truce, true, and rue ; u in Muth ; ou in roule … … … …	出	父
û	u in butt … … … …	風	同
ŭ	u in buse ; û in Bühne … …	去	均

II. Diphthongs and Triphthongs.

These are described invariably by a coalition of the simple vowels of this orthography, *each* of which must be sounded in the manner shown in the preceding table. Some are dwelt on longer than the others, but it would be useless to attempt to describe this by diacritical marks.

Diphthong or Triphthong of New Orthography.	Examples in Chinese.	Diphthong or Triphthong of New Orthography.	Examples in Chinese.
ai	來 白	ie	雞 寫
au	少 道	ieu	酒 九
ea	兩 諒	iê	業 別
eau	料 了	iô	覓 學
eê	連 臉	ôu	肉 口
ei	為 貴	ŏi	雷 內
eô	畧 黑	ui	追 隨
ėi	飛 價	ûi	罪 水
ia	下 叫	ŭê	摧 選
iau	小		

III. Consonants.

Consonant of New Orthog.	Homophonous Sounds in the English, French, or German Languages.	Examples in Chinese.	
ch	ch in channel, Chester … …	站	毚
ch'	The preceding sound with an aspiration	昌	起
chw	chw in churchwarden, catchword …	窓	柴
chw'	The preceding sound with an aspiration	床	撞
f	f in fan, fun … … … …	翻	父
ğ	Resembling the g in gun; but in forming the sound, the tongue must not be pressed against the palate …	恩	
gh	ch in the Scotch Loch Lomond; ch in Chemie and in sprechen … …	和	海
ghw	The preceding guttural sound immediately followed by the English wh, as heard in when … … …	會	黄 縣
h̆s	A sound between that of s in see and sh in she … … … …	心	人
j̆	Resembling the French j in jaune, but with much less of the buzzing sound	日	
j̆w	The preceding sound, with a full English w immediately after it …	軟	該
k	k in kalendar … … …	高	開
k'	The preceding sound with an aspiration	恐	官
kw	qu in quack, queen … … …	廣	

III. Consonants (*continued*).

Consonant of New Orthog.	Homophonous Sounds in the English, French, or German Languages.	Examples in Chinese.
kw'	The preceding sound with an aspiration	快 憒
l	l in land, lee, lay, lungs	冷 李
lw	lw in bulwark, hellward	亂 鑾
m	m in man, me, may	帽 米
n	n in nab, need, nun	拏 内
nw	nw in Cornwall	煖 暖
p	p in pan, pun, pang	筆 辨
p	The preceding sound with an aspiration	派 皮
r	*Resembling* the r in demur; but the sound is prolonged. In forming this sound (which only occurs after û) the tip of the tongue must not touch the palate	耳 二
s	s in sand, see	三 所
sh	sh in shun; ſch in ſchanbe; ch in chamois	啇 手
shw	The preceding sound with a full English w immediately after it; ſchw in Schwan, Schwur	說 水
sw	sw in swan	筭 酸
t	t in tan, tingle, tongue, tun ...	大 頂
t'	The preceding sound with an aspiration	他 太

III. Consonants (*continued*).

Consonant of New Orthog.	Homophonous sounds in the English, French, or German Languages.	Examples in Chinese.
ts	ts in Whi*ts*untide; ʒ in Ʒaɦn, Ʒinn, ʒu	早 子
ts'	{ The preceding sound with an aspi-ration ... ... }	草 此
tsw	{ The above sound of ts with a full English w immediately after it; ʒw in Ʒwang ... ... }	鑽
tsw'	The preceding sound with an aspiration	纂
tw	tw in twang	段 短 搏
tw'	The preceding sound with an aspiration	圍 王
w	w in wag, wan	外 羊
y	y in year, yes	應

NOTE VI.

ON THE INTONATIONS OR TONES CALLED SHĔNG
BY THE CHINESE.

THIS is a subject which puzzles the beginner
very much, not merely in Europe, but even in
China.

I shall be happy if what I now say about it
should save any one the trouble of racking his
brains on the matter; and, as it will doubtless
add some weight to my opinions, and give them
more authority, I would beg the reader to bear
in mind, that I am daily forced, in the discharge
of my duties, to put them to a practical test.

The difficulty is threefold: first, to discover
what these shĕng, on which so much has been
written of a directly contradictory nature, possibly
can be; secondly, whether it is, or is not, useful,
important, or indispensably necessary, to acquire
a knowledge of them; and thirdly, to what extent, and in what manner, that knowledge should
be acquired.

1. The shĕng are not produced by any alteration of the vowel sound,* for sounds which we

* I speak solely with reference to the Pekin, or court, pro-

can only write with one and the same vowel, as, for instance, a in fang, fan, u in chu, are pronounced with all the different shĕng; they are not formed by any modification of the consonants, for in words which contain no consonants at all, the shĕng are perhaps most distinctly heard; neither do they consist in quickness or slowness, i. e. in a change of the duration of time taken to pronounce the words; and still less do they consist in loudness or lowness, i. e. that alteration which renders a sound audible at a distance, or only close at hand. The shĕng are produced solely by the sinking, rising, or non-alteration of the sound, as it would stand in the gamut; i. e. supposing a word to be pitched at B, it will, with some of the shĕng, rise higher in the scale, to C, D, or E; with others it will maintain the B; and with others again, it will sink to A and G. It even seems to me, that the shĕng give the words an *absolute* place in the gamut; i. e. that certain words, when properly pronounced with their shĕng, should, for instance, always commence with C, and rise gradually to E, and that if pitched at B, and made to rise to D, they cease, to a Chinese ear, to be the word intended, and either become

nunciation, in which the shĕng differ materially from those in the Canton and Fuchiên dialects. In the court pronunciation, only four shĕng are heard; in the Nankin, five; and in the Canton and Fuchiên, seven or eight.

another word of the language, or no word at all. This is particularly perceptible in the Canton pronunciation of the provincial dialect; and if any one will listen to a coolie talking, he cannot fail to observe how the successive sounds take wide leaps up and down the gamut.

It is evident from the above, that a good practical musician could elucidate the matter very much to his brethren;* but as the shĕng must, after all, be acquired by listening to, and imitating, the Chinese, what I have said above, together with the following remarks and table, is probably quite sufficient on the subject, serving, as it will, to show the beginner to what he ought to confine his attention.

Morrison, in his Grammar, gives five shĕng for the colloquial, as spoken by the mandarins; viz., the shang pîng, hsia pîng, shang, chŭ, and ju; which he calls the upper even, the lower even, the high, the going, and the entering; and marks them respectively by — ∧ ＼ ／ ∪. He adds, however, that in the Pekin dialect the short tones (meaning thereby the entering ones, marked ∪) "are lengthened, or rather, do not exist." According to Morrison, then, the shĕng of the Pekin, or court, pronunciation are four, the upper even, the lower even, the high, and the going;

* The late Mr. Dyer, missionary in the Straits, has, I believe, done this in one of his works.

which is precisely what I have found to be the case. In some few words the natives of Pekin shorten the sound abruptly, or make use of the entering shĕng; but these words are exceptions to the general rule, and should be individually remembered as such.

A TABLE OF THE SHĔNG, OR CHINESE INTONATIONS USED IN THE COURT PRONUNCIATION;

Giving their names, an attempt to describe them, some Examples for practice with a Teacher, and the Number used in this Volume, as well as the Marks used by Morrison to distinguish them.

聲 Shĕng, or Intonations.	Description.	Examples.	Marked in this Book by	Marks used by Morrison.
上平 shang ping, first even	Commences at a high note, and keeps high and even ...	韋 青 非 灰 鄉 姑	1	—
下平 hsia ping, second even	Commences at a high note, and rises still higher ...	常 情 肥 回 祥 骨	2	⟨
上 shang, rising ...	Commences at a low note, and rises to a higher one ...	掌 請 匪 跛 宰 畝	3	╱
去 chŭ, departing ...	Commences at a low note, and sinks still lower ...	帳 慶 廢 會 向 顧	4	╲

2. As to the use, importance, or absolute necessity, of acquiring a knowledge of the shĕng.
On this subject many conflicting opinions have
been given; and I well remember how much I
was, in consequence, puzzled, at the commencement of my studies, to decide whether I should
or should not devote any time,—a valuable thing
to the student of Chinese,—in order to make myself master of them. I consulted both books and
living scholars, in Europe and in China. Some
seemed to say, that the shĕng are of no use whatsoever; others, that they are useful only to the
man who wishes to write Chinese poetry; others,
again, that they are generally useful, but that it
is impossible for foreigners to learn them; and
some go even so far as to say, that a man cannot
speak Chinese unless he be able to tell, when he
sees each Chinese character, with what intonation
it is to be pronounced.

Now the truth seems to lie, as it has been
found to do in the case of so many other contested
points, between the extreme opinions. I venture
to say, that no foreigner ever was, and none will
ever be, able to tell, from memory alone, the
proper intonations of each of the 10,000 characters *commonly* used, when placed *written* before
him; and, on the other hand, if *in speaking* you
do not give the characters used the proper intonation, you are perpetually liable to be misunder-

stood, and will frequently make most ludicrous mistakes. I give an instance or two of the latter from my own experience.

In making out a report to the superintendent of customs, of the export cargo of a ship about to leave, I took the English manifest, and read aloud, in Chinese, the various articles to a clerk, who was sitting by me with his writing implements. The last species of goods, of a very large cargo, happened to be "vitrified ware." This is called, tǔ shàu leàu, in Chinese; I, however, gave a wrong intonation, and said, tǔ shàu leàu, whereupon the Chinese instantly lifted his hand from the paper, and looked at me with surprise, and only stared the more, when I repeated the words,—with great reason, too, for I was in fact deliberately and distinctly telling him, that the large and very valuable cargo I had just enumerated, had been "all burnt up," such being the only meaning of the three words I uttered.

On another occasion, I said something to a Chinese of "bargain money," or "earnest money," as I thought. As he did not seem to understand, I repeated the words; upon which he thrust forward his head, and listened attentively, and the louder I spoke, the nearer he came, anxiously turning one side of his head towards me, to catch the sound. In fact, instead of saying tîng ch'ièn,

F

bargain money, I was shouting, t'ĭng chiĕn, t'ĭng
chiĕn, do you hear! do you hear!

The use of an improper shĕng makes, in reality,
a much greater difference to the ear of a Chinese
than an alteration of the vowel, or consonantal
sound. A word, for instance, which we write
lĭng, may be pronounced as if written lĭng, lĭn,
nĭng, nĭng, and nĭn, or one written tsŭng, may be
pronounced chŭng, chung, chŭn, and a Chinese
would understand perfectly well; but if the words
lĭng and tsŭng be pronounced lĭng and tsŭng, he
instantly understands thereby characters different
from those it was intended to use, and is consequently unable to comprehend the speaker. The
above instances are sufficient to prove, that it is
absolutely necessary, in *speaking* Chinese, to give
the proper intonations to the characters; and I
could give many more, either from my own early
experience, or such as might occur daily in the
common intercourse of life. A different intonation is, in truth, a different word, and therefore
you cannot be said to speak Chinese, unless you
give the proper intonation, any more than a German would be said to speak English who would
say, " I became a pistol," when intending to say,
" I got a louis d'or" (Ich bekam eine Piſtole); or,
" We struck ourselves upon pistols," instead of,
" We fought a duel with pistols " (Wir ſchlugen
uns auf Piſtolen). Both of these expressions have

been actually made use of to me, and I was as much puzzled to conceive what my German friends meant, as my Chinese acquaintances doubtless were to conceive my meaning in the above quoted instances.

Few of the Chinese can *name* the shĕng with which the characters ought to be pronounced; but none of them ever use a wrong one, when called on to pronounce the characters themselves, and in so far they are, therefore, infallible guides.

3. As to what extent, and in what manner, a knowledge of the shĕng should be acquired.

If the student be unable to procure a good teacher, or if he do not intend learning to speak, but merely to read the written character, then the less attention he pays to every thing connected with the pronunciation the better. But if he desire to study the spoken language, and have at hand a teacher whose *native* pronunciation is that particular one he desires to acquire, then his first business should be, to make the teacher repeat, and carefully to repeat after him, characters belonging to each of the four shĕng; and he should continue to do this until able to refer, without hesitation, every Chinese word he hears distinctly pronounced by a Chinese, to its proper shĕng. When he has advanced thus far, he should commence repeating, always after the teacher,

words and sentences, in a loud voice, taking care
to pronounce them exactly as the latter does, but
without stopping to reflect what shĕng they have.
It would be in vain to attempt to retain in the
memory what particular shĕng each word is pronounced with, and although, as is stated above, a
man cannot be said to speak Chinese who uses
improper shĕng, yet a practically useful command
of them is only to be attained by calling in the
assistance to be derived from mere mechanical
habit.   The words must be repeated again and
again, after a teacher, first singly, and then in
sentences, until the organs of speech have become
so habituated to the pronouncing of a certain
character in one certain manner, as always to pronounce it in that manner, and consequently with
the proper shĕng, without requiring any exertion
of the reflection or memory on the part of the
speaker.

    The principal reason for learning, as I have
recommended, so much of the shĕng as to be able
to recognize and pronounce them as soon as
heard, is, that the student thereby becomes better
able to imitate the teacher.   Unless he push his
knowledge of them so far, he will, in reading
after his teacher, find the latter correcting on one
word a dozen times in succession, without his
being able to discover wherein his mistake lies.
And when he at length does stumble on the

right intonation, he will, if required to pronounce
the word once more, most probably not be able
to do so, but go on making his former mistakes.
It was the great loss of time which I experienced
in this way myself, at the commencement of my
studies, that first convinced me of the necessity
of learning to distinguish the shĕng.   There are,
however, other occasions on which this knowledge
of them becomes useful.   For instance, if in talking to a Chinese you give a character a wrong
shĕng, and he in consequence do not comprehend
you, by pronouncing the same character, as represented by our letters, with each of the four shĕng
successively, you are sure of pronouncing it in the
proper manner in, at the most, four trials; and
when you do, the Chinaman generally understands you at once.   A friend of mine was, after
he had studied according to the above plan for a
few months, frequently obliged to have recourse
to this expedient in giving orders to his servant;
but he thus made himself understood where he
would otherwise have been obliged to remain altogether silent.

    In concluding this note on the shĕng it is ne-
cessary to remark to the beginner, that the Chinese have also got an aspirate, marked usually by
an (') following the aspirated consonant; and that
in imitating a teacher it is consequently necessary
to attend to four things, the shĕng, the vowel

sounds, the consonantal sounds, and the aspirate, without which it will often be impossible to perceive wherein his corrections lie. It will generally be found that the aspirate is the most difficult to distinguish, but it is in many cases of as much importance as the shĕng.

Departments	1st Circuit named Kwang-shan-nan lwin Kwang-sham-nan-fan	Districts	N.º	Departments	2nd Circuit named Chwui-chau-chia Hwuy-chau-kai	Districts	N.º	Departments	3rd Circuit named Shau-lo Shaou-lo	Districts	N.º	Departments	4th Circuit named Kau-lwin Kaou-lien	Districts	N.º	Departments	5th Circuit named Loi-chiung Luy-kiung	Districts	N.º
KWANG CHÖI Kwang-chau		Nan-hai Nan-hae	1			Kwei-shan Kwei-shan	26			Kau-yau Kaou-yaou	51			Mou-ming Maou-ming	67			Chai-kang Hae-kang	76
		Pun-yü Pwan-yu	2			Pö-lö Po-lo	27			Si-ghwui Sze-hwuy	52			Tiên-pö Teen-pih	68	LOI CHÖI Luy-chau		Sui-chi Suy-khe	77
		Shün-tö Shun-tih	3			Chang-ning Chang-ning	28			Hsin-hsing Sin-hing	53			Hsin-i Sin-i	69			Hsi-wän Sei-wan	78
		Tüng-kwan Tung-kwan	4			Ying-an Yung-gan	29	SHAU CHÖI Shaou-chau		Yang-chün Yang-chun	54			Chau-chau (chau) Haou-chau	70			Chiung-shan Kiung-shan	79
KWANG CHÖI Kwang-chau		Tsüng-ghwa Tsang-hwa	5	CHWUI CHÖI Hwuy-chau		Chai-füng Hae-fung	30			Yang-chang Yang-kiang	55			Nu-chwan Nee-chuen	71			Ching-mai Ching-mae	80
		Lung-mün Lung-mun	6			Lui-füng Luy-fung	31			Kau-ming Kaou-ming	56			Sui-chüng Suy-chung	72			Ting-an Ting-gan	81
		Hsin-ning Sin-ning	7			Lüng-chwan Lung-chuen	32	LÖ TING Lo-ting		Gün-ping Gan-ping	57			Chi-pu Hi-poo	73			Wan-chang Wan-chang	82
		Tsang-ching Tsang-ching	8			Lien-ping Leen-ping	33			Kwang-ning Kwang-ning	58	LÖEN CHÖI Leen-chau		Chü-chwui Hae-chuen	74			Ghwui-ting Hwuy-tung	83
		Hsiang-shan Heang-shan	9			Chö-yuen Ho-yuen	34			Kü-ping Kuh-ping	59			Ling-shan Ling-shan	75			Tai-chang Ta-chang	84
		Hsin-chwui Sin-hwuy	10			Chö-ping Ho-ping	35			Chau-shan Chaou-shan	60							Lö-ghwui Lo-hwuy	85
		San-shwui Sam-shwuy	11			Chai-yang Hae-yang	36			To-ching Tih-khing	61					CHÜ-SU-CHÖI Kiung-chau		Lin-kau Lin-kaou	86
SHAT CHÖI Shaou-chau		Ching-yuen Tsing-yuen	12			Füng-shun Fung-shun	37			Füng-chwan Fung-chuen	62							Tan (chöi) Tan-chau	87
		Hsin-an Sin-gan	13	CHAI CHÖI Chaou-chau		Chau-yang Chaou-yang	38			Kai-chien Kae-keen	63							Chang-ghwa Chang-hwa	88
		Ghwui-chwun Hwuy-chau	14			Chai-yang Kee-yang	39			Lö-ting Lo-ting	64							Wan (chöi) Wan-chau	89
NAN HSIUNG Nan-hsiung		Chü-chiang Khuh-keang	15			Jau-ping Yaou-ping	40			Ting-an Ting-gan	65							Lö-ghwui Ling-shwui	90
		Lö-chang Lo-chang	16	CHAI YING Kee-ying		Ghwui-lai Hwuy-lae	41			Hsi-ming Se-ming	66							Ni (chau) Ya-chau	91
		Jön-ghwa Jin-hwa	17			Jau-ping Yaou-ping	42											Kan-gün Kan-gan	
		Ju-yuen Joo-yuen	18			Ta-pü Ta-poo	43												
LÖEN CHÖI Leen-chau		Wäng-yuen Ong-yuen	19			Chāng-ghwa Chang-lo	44												
		Ying-tö Ying-tih	20			Pu-ning Poo-ning	45												
		Nan-hsiung Nan-hsiung	21			Chia-ying Keang-ying	46												
LÖEN SHAN Leen-shan		Lian-chöi Leen-chau	22	WÖ KÖNG Fuh-kang		Chang-lö Chang-lo	47												
		Lö-chöi Leen-chau	23			Hsing-ning Hing-ning	48												
		Lian-shan Leen-shan	24			Ping-yuen Ping-yuen	49												
		Lian-shan Leen-shan	25			Chen-ping Chin-ping	50												

The material originally positioned here is too large for reproduction in this reissue. A PDF can be downloaded from the web address given on page iv of this book, by clicking on 'Resources Available'.

The material originally positioned here is too large for reproduction in this reissue. A PDF can be downloaded from the web address given on page iv of this book, by clicking on 'Resources Available'.

NOTE VII.

SKETCH OF KWANG-TUNG.

THE adjoining sketch of the province of Kwang-tung has been compiled entirely from maps contained in the Chinese work entitled Kwang-tung tung chĭ,* with the exception, however, of the line of coast extending from the mouth of the Canton river eastward to the province of Fuchiên, in sketching which I have in some measure followed European maps. In making the sketch, I paid little or no attention to the Chinese map of the province, or to those of the departments, but have compiled it from the district maps; just as if I had, for instance, drawn a map of England on a small scale from large maps of the individual counties. It was at first my intention to have drawn a map, and on a much larger scale, but I found so many discrepancies between the maps of the different districts, when I attempted to delineate their common boundaries, that I was soon obliged to give up the idea. It would seem that the latitude and longitude of the district cities

* " General Account of Kwang-tung." It is usually stitched in 140 Chinese volumes.

only had been ascertained by observations, and
not even the longitude of these always. The
positions of all the other places in the districts
seem to have been ascertained—if, indeed, they
have been ascertained at all—not from a trigono-
metrical net of triangles, but from some direct
measurement, like our surveying by the chain.
Now as the districts are about the size of English
counties, it is evident no great correctness could
be attained in this way, even if the work were
executed by good English surveyors of the present day; and when I tell my readers, in addition to this, the Chinese surveyors do not even
seem to have understood the plan of taking the
base distances, but have manifestly run their lines
close along the surface of the ground, up hill and
down dale, they will perceive that the boundary
line of each district map must overlap those of
the surrounding districts. This is, in fact, almost
invariably the case. I could, therefore, only compile the sketch by *fudging*; and, though the
fudging has been done according to one fixed
rule, viz. by proportioning the reduction in the
extent of the boundaries to their distances from
their respective district cities, and to the apparent
nature of the surface, still it must contain many
errors. I trust, however, it will be found of some
interest, as displaying the civil divisions of the
province.

Many of the smaller branches of rivers contained in the Chinese maps have not been given again. Thus the Shûn tŏ district is literally a collection of river islands, from the number of water passages which intersect it, but I have not attempted to delineate any of the latter.

In the table which accompanies the sketch, the names of all the circuits, departments, and districts are given twice; first according to the court pronunciation, and in a new orthography, and then as written by Morrison.

NOTE VIII.

ON THE RANK, DUTIES, AND SALARIES OF THE
MANDARINS.

OBJECTIONS have been made, by parties whose
opinions are entitled to respect, to the use of the
word "mandarin" as a designation of the Chinese
officers: I am, however, inclined to join with
those who would retain it, for, apart from the
consideration of its long use in this signification,
the Chinese officers, being a large and very peculiar body of men, are well entitled to a peculiar
designation, and it is rather to be regarded as a
convenience that they should have one. The
term should, however, only be employed with
reference to those whose names are entered in
"The Red Book," and to those who have been
accepted as "expectants," or "candidates," by the
government at Pekin; and it should by no means
be applied to every man who wears a button, or
to the clerks and other persons employed in the
Yamun. I have retained the term, with the re-
striction just mentioned, throughout these Notes.

The mandarins may be divided, according to
the nature of their duties, into three grand orders;
viz., 1st, the civil; 2nd, the literary (who super-

intend the examinations); and 3rd, the military.
In the present Note I shall first make a few observations about the division into classes common
to all three orders, and about their uniforms, and
then proceed to give a short description of the
provincial civilians. With most of these latter
we have frequent transactions, and their titles
will consequently come daily more before the
public; while, at the same time, not one European in ten thousand has the most remote idea
of the nature and extent of their respective functions. With the ministers at the capital we have,
as yet, no intercourse; and we have little or no
communication with the literary and the military
mandarins in the provinces.

The mandarins of all the three orders mentioned above are divided into nine classes, each
class distinguished from the others by a peculiar
uniform, the most characteristic part of which is
the button. Each of these classes is again sub-
divided into a first and a secondary division, without, however, any difference in the uniform. To
these nine classes we may add another of mandarins whom the Chinese call wi ju lieu, " not yet
entered the stream," i. e. unclassed; their uniform is the same as that of the ninth class. This
classification is merely one of *rank*, hence the
button, as part of the uniform, does not indicate
the particular office of the wearer, nor even show

his true standing as a mandarin; for a district magistrate, for instance, who by his office belongs to the seventh class, and wears a gilt button, is in reality higher, i. e. holds a more lucrative and more influential post, than the secretary of a provincial superintendent of finances, who, as such secretary, belongs to the sixth class, and wears a white button.

The peacock's feather has nothing to do with this classification, it being, like the European orders, always especially granted to the individual wearer.

The full dress uniforms are described at length in the above mentioned "Red Book;" but the following particulars respecting the buttons worn on the apex of the caps contain all the information that is ever likely to be useful to Europeans.

On ordinary occasions, the mandarins of the different classes wear:

1st class,   a plain red button.
2nd „   a flowered ditto.
3rd „   a transparent blue button.
4th „   an opaque ditto.
5th „   an uncoloured glass button.
6th „   a white ditto.
7th „   a plain gilt button.
8th „   a gilt button with flowers in relief.
9th „ & }
Unclassed, }   a gilt button with engraved flowers.

J.R Jobbins del.

A MANDARIN OF THE SIXTH CLASS IN SUMMER HALF DRESS UNIFORM.

Published by W.H.Allen & Cº Leadenhall Street. March 1847.

J.R Jobbins del.

A MANDARIN OF THE SIXTH CLASS IN WINTER HALF DRESS UNIFORM.

Published by W.H.Allen & C? Leadenhall Street. March 1847.

A MANDARIN OF THE FOURTH CLASS IN FULL DRESS UNIFORM; WINTER CAP.

Published by W.H.Allen & Cº Leadenhall Street. March 1847.

The mandarins, from the first to the fifth classes inclusive, wear a chaplet of beads round the neck. A conical cap, on which these buttons are fixed, and from the apex of which strings of red silk, or red hair, fall down on all sides nearly to the lower rim, together with a pair of wide black satin boots, and a gown gathered round the waist by a girdle, forms what we would consider the *half-dress* uniform of a mandarin. It is represented in the first of the adjoining lithographs. There is no fixed colour for the gown, but a reddish brown grass-cloth is generally worn in summer, and in winter blue silks prevail, over which fur pelisses are frequently worn, as is shown in the second plate. The succeeding lithographs give an idea of the full-dress uniform of the mandarins, which they, among themselves, wear on occasions similar to those on which foreigners wear their full-dress uniforms ; but they seldom appear in them when they visit barbarians. On the square of cloth in the front and back, the civil and literary mandarins have birds, the military, beasts, depicted.

They have a third plainer dress, called chau i, or court garments, which is only worn on the most solemn occasions, having reference to the Imperial family.

In describing the civilians of the provinces, I shall take as an example-those of Kwang-tung, which contains nearly every description of mandarin that is to be found in any other. I have not been able to find any Chinese book expressly treating of the particular duties of the different mandarins of the present day, and have, therefore, been obliged to collect my information partly by extracting it from the Penal Code, and the Code of the Board of Civil Office,—the laws and regulations of which works occasionally throw light on the extent and nature of the powers exercised by officials,—partly from short notices and notes on the subject contained in the "Ta ching ghwui tièn, Institutions of the Chinese Empire," and in "The Red Book;"* partly from my own experience in the transaction of the consular business; and a good deal by conversation with the mandarins, their secretaries, and clerks; and though the information thus acquired may appear to the reader but scanty, I can assure him the task of collecting it has been sufficiently difficult. For instance, when you ask a Chinese, "What sort of

* The works mentioned here contain a multitude of minute regulations regarding the selection, promotion, and degradation of the mandarins, their obtaining leave of absence on account of sickness, or for the purpose of mourning the death of their parents, &c. &c.; but very little concerning the duties incumbent on them. What they do contain, too, on this latter head, frequently differs widely from what actually exists in practice, a circumstance that materially increases the difficulty attendant on the investigation of the subject.

business does a Tau tai transact?" the usual answer is, " Um—why he transacts a Tau tai's business." "Yes," you rejoin, varying your expressions, "but I want to know what particular kind
of public business it is peculiarly his province to
manage?" "Ah! ah! I understand, why—why
—all kinds of public business."

And this is, in fact, the most important truth
you ascertain, namely, that a Chinese mandarin
is supposed to be capable of transacting all kinds
of public affairs,—at least such of them as have
attained the second literary grade of Chŭ jĕn.
The lowest post then given the candidate is that
of a district magistrate, an office in which the
functions and powers of the judicial body, the
police, and the fiscal department are united; he
is thus, as it were, at once judge, sheriff, director
of police, and collector of taxes; and he continues, as he gets promotion, to act in all the different departments, either at one time, or successively. This must be constantly borne in mind
in reading the following attempt to show what
are the more peculiar duties of each provincial
mandarin. These I shall, for the sake of perspi-
cuity, treat of under thirteen heads.

1. Tsûng tu, the Governor-general.

This is the highest civilian in the province of
Kwang-tung, of which, and its sister province,

Kwang-hsi, he is the governor-general.* His powers and duties are much like those of the governor of a British colony, so much so, as to render any enumeration of them unnecessary ; but to form a proper idea of his standing, it must be kept in mind that the above named two provinces, over which he exercises so great an authority, are together as large an extent of territory, and contain a greater population, than Great Britain and Ireland, taken together with German Prussia. The governor-general belongs to the first class of mandarins, by his ex officio dignity of president of the Board of War, a dignity by virtue of which he is enabled to command the military of the two provinces. It is like the dignity of commander-in-chief, as held by the governors of our colonies. As governor-general, he exercises authority over the civil mandarins and the people.

The present governor-general of Kwang-tung and Kwang-hsi is Chî yîng, a Manchoo of high standing, who was chief of the commission that concluded the treaty of peace at Nankin; and has since, in his capacity of imperial commissioner for

---

* He (as well as the officer next described, the Fu tai) has been called " viceroy," but this title seems latterly to have given place to the better one of governor-general. By the seamen at Whampoa he is entitled " John Tuck," a corruption of Tsûng tu, which latter word is pronounced tuk in the Canton dialect.

foreign commercial affairs, which he still retains, negotiated the treaties with America and France.

2. Fu Tai, the Governor.

This is the second civilian of the province of Kwang-tûng, of which he is governor. This title is sometimes rendered by " lieutenant-governor," but this does not seem to give an adequate idea of his powers. He has, as ex officio vice-president of the Board of War, a certain number of troops under his command, altogether independent of the governor-general,—the latter must consult with him on all matters of any importance, relating to the province of Kwang-tûng,— in certain cases, which are sufficiently numerous, he issues a death-warrant, just as the governor-general does; and, like the latter, he can at all times send a report direct to the Emperor on any subject, a privilege that would alone place him almost on a virtual equality with the governor-general, where there is so much to conceal, and so many stories to make up. His duties, therefore, are also very much like those of the governor of an English colony ; the powers implied by that title being, to a certain extent, divided between him and the governor-general. A distinction in the nature of their duties that the Chinese always make, when questioned on the subject, is, that the governor-general is almost exclusively concerned in what passes on the rivers and the sea, while the governor is more immediately concerned with what passes on the land.

The present governor of Kwang-tûng, Ghwang găn tûng, a highly talented Chinese, has been associated with Chi yîng, in all his dealings with the foreigners, since the commencement of negotiations at Nankin ; and the latter, it is said here, defers greatly to his opinion, both in foreign and home affairs.

3. FAN TAI, THE SUPERINTENDENT OF FINANCES.

This is the third mandarin whose authority extends over the whole province. He is usually called " the treasurer," but this is, I think, a more inadequate term than that of " superintendent of finances;" for he has himself a treasurer, a mandarin of the eighth class, with considerable emoluments and a separate establishment. The superintendent of finances receives that part of the land tax which is fixed in money, from the district magistrates and other local authorities. They pay it directly into his establishment, and he has, consequently, from the way in which these things are done in China, a great influence over them. He has, besides, the privilege of addressing the Emperor directly three times in the year. On two of these occasions the address is said to be merely a congratulatory form, but on

the third he makes a long report on all the affairs
of the province.

The standards of weights and measures are
deposited in his yamun. He pays the salaries of
all the mandarins, and those newly appointed
must deliver their credentials to him. Besides
these, his peculiar duties, he exercises, under the
governor-general and the governor, a general
superintendence over all the affairs of the province.

4. NIÊ TAI, THE PROVINCIAL JUDGE.

This is the next mandarin. In criminal cases
he may be called the highest judicial authority of
the province; for, although the governor-general
and the governor, in granting a death-warrant,
also re-examine the criminal, it is merely for
form's sake, and not in the hope, or with the
intention, of throwing any new light on the case.
The judge is the officer usually deputed to quell
tumults and rebellions against the mandarins in
distant parts of the province, on which occasions
he has the power delegated to him of issuing
death-warrants; and having then the chief command of the troops that accompany him, the
square of cloth he wears on his full-dress uniform
has a beast depicted on it, the mark of a military
mandarin. In addition to the criminal jurisdiction, which is especially his province, he can take

cognizance of civil actions. He has also the general control of the imperial post in Kwangtûng. Besides these duties, he is, in accordance with what is said above,* frequently appointed by the governor-general or the governor to deliberate with his immediate superior, the superintendent of finances, on matters relating to the general government of the province, such as the abrogation of prohibitions, the establishment of new regulations, &c. &c.

He has the privilege of addressing the Emperor, in the same manner as the superintendent of finances.

5. YŬN TAI, THE COLLECTOR OF THE SALT GABEL, OR THE SALT COMMISSIONER.

This is the fifth civilian of the province, and the only one, besides the governor-general, whose authority extends to Kwang hši. That authority is, however, confined to the salt department, and a superintendence over the sale of native iron, which he manages by the aid of his own subalterns, independent of the district magistrates. Of these subaltern mandarins there are eighteen, from the fourth to the eighth class inclusive, distributed throughout the provinces of Kwang-tûng and Kwang hši, and some of the adjoining departments of Chiang hsi, Ghu nan, and Fu chiên, to

* See page 80.

which adjoining departments the authority of the salt commissioner also extends.

6. LEANG CHU TAU, THE GRAIN COLLECTOR.

This is the lowest of the mandarins whose operations extend over the whole province of Kwang-tûng. His duty is to superintend the collection of that part of the land tax which is fixed payable in kind, or to name the price and receive the amount of so much as may ultimately be demanded in money. He also acts as a kind of commissary-general, superintending the distribution of their rations to the military throughout the province.

7. TAU TAI, THE INTENDANT OF CIRCUIT.

There are five of these in the province, one being stationed in each of the five circuits into which, as a reference to the " Sketch of Kwang-tûng " and the annexed table will shew, it is unequally divided. While the offices of superintendent of finances, of provincial judge, of salt commissioner, and of grain collector, have, to a certain degree, each a particular class of duties attached to them, the office of intendant unites in itself, in a manner similar to that of governor-general and that of governor, a direct general superintendence over all the affairs of a circuit, not excluding those of a military nature. The only difference seems to be, that the intendant, as a lower officer, with his attention confined to a smaller territory, must go more into the details, while in matters of importance he must refer to the judge, or to the superintendent of finances, or both, according to the nature of the case. Like all his superiors, with the exception of the judge, he has no prisons under his immediate control; on the other hand, he has corn stores, and seems, like the grain collector, to have some part of the commissariat duties to discharge. An intendant may get promotion, either to the post of salt commissioner or to that of provincial judge; or he may be made grain collector, which is, however, not called a promotion, inasmuch as he ranks as high as this latter officer.

8. Chǐ fu, prefect of department; chǐ li chóu, prefect of inferior department; and chǐ li tûng chǐ, independent sub-prefect.

There are in Kwang-tûng nine chǐ fu, each having the general superintendence of one of the nine fu, or departments, contained in the province;* four chǐ li chôu, one at the head of each of the inferior departments denominated chôu, viz. Chia yîng chôu, Nan-chiûng chôu, Leên chôu, and Lô-tîng chôu; and two chǐ-li-tûng-chǐ, one

* See Sketch of Kwang-tûng, which was drawn chiefly with the view of serving as an illustration to this Note.

at the head of each of the inferior departments denominated tîng, viz. Leên-shan tîng and Fô-kang tîng. The duties of these three descriptions of mandarins are the same in their nature, and the only difference subsisting between them is, that the prefect of inferior department and the independent sub-prefect have a smaller territory under them, and are *promoted* to the post of prefect. The two former are, however, in their respective posts, not placed under any prefect; but when they have occasion to refer to a superior, they communicate directly with the intendant in whose circuit their departments are situated, or to the higher provincial authorities.

What I have said about the nature of the intendant's duties is again applicable here, the prefects and independent sub-prefects exercising a general control over all the public affairs of their departments. They seem, however, to have less concern than the intendants with the commissariat and financial affairs. On the other hand, they have much business of a judicial nature, and have all prisons under their immediate authority.

The inferior departments, called chĭ-li tîng, are, in point of territorial extent, not larger than the districts or subdivisions of those departments called fu and chĭ-li chôu; but independent sub-prefects are stationed in them, on account of circumstances which make the administration of affairs unusually difficult, and render it expedient to have an officer of higher rank than a district magistrate always at hand.

Thus the inferior department of Leên-shan contains a great number of mountaineers, like the Highlanders, or the Kerry Irish, called Yau, whence the sub-prefect has the two words Li-yau i. e. "ruling the yau," prefixed to his title.

9. Tûng chǐ, sub-prefect; and Tûng pan, deputy sub-prefect.

Of the former, there are eight in Kwang-tûng, of the latter, seven. With the exception of one sub-prefect placed under the salt commissioner (in which post he *ranks* as high as a prefect), and of a deputy sub-prefect, who assists the grain collector, all these officers are stationed at different important points through the province : at military stations, many of them having the power to set troops in motion ; at large towns ; and in the neighbourhood of mountaineers, or of places frequented by "outer barbarians." Thus there is a sub-prefect at the large manufacturing town of Fo shan, near Canton ; one at Chiên-shan, near Macao (mandarin of Casa Branca) ; and one at Yai chôu, in Ghai-nan, a district that is said to be " suspended, orphanlike, at the extreme south, with the vast and boundless ocean on three sides, and the Li mountaineers on the borders to be tranquillized and guided."

They are also a sort of sheriffs-general for several districts, having the duty incumbent on them of apprehending criminals in these districts.

The sub-prefecture of Chiê shǐ, a military station near the coast, in the Lu fûng district in the Ghwûi chŏu department, was, a few months ago, removed to the Bocca Tigris.*

In the inferior departments, called Chǐ-li chôu, there are CHÔU TÛNG, sub-prefects, and CHÔU PAN, deputy sub-prefects, of inferior departments, who are employed much in the same way as the corresponding officers of the superior departments.

10. CHǏ CHÔU AND CHǏ HSIÊN, DISTRICT MAGISTRATES.

The two Chinese titles are rendered into English by one common term, for although the mandarin bearing the first title *ranks* higher, belonging to the fifth class, while the chǐ hsiên belongs to the seventh, yet in every other respect they are equal, their duties and powers being exactly alike. They take their titles from the names of their districts, just as if, in England, the sheriffs of

* The island of Chusan is the station of a sub-prefect. This island, with the smaller neighbouring ones, forms a district called Tˈing ghai, the name by which it is always spoken of by the mandarins among themselves, and which it bears in all the works published by Imperial authority.

all those counties to which the syllable "shire" is not attached, were, with the same powers and duties as at present, to be entitled "counts" of counties, and be ranked higher than the "sheriffs" of shires.

As said above, at page 79, the district magistrate is at once judge, collector of taxes, director of police, and sheriff of his district.

His yamun is the court of first instance, in all cases,* for the Chinese law prohibits, under penalty of fifty blows with the lesser bamboo, any application to a prefect, or other superior mandarin, till the district magistrate has either given, or declined giving, a decision; while, on the other hand, if his subalterns, the assistant district magistrates, township magistrates, &c. &c., take cognizance of any criminal case or action at law themselves, instead of referring it to their superior, as soon as brought to their notice, they are, by the Code of the Board of Civil Office, to be degraded one step, and removed from their posts; and if they venture to take up any case, criminal or civil, and there should be a subsequent loss of human life in connection with it, they are to be cashiered.

---

* It takes the place, both in criminal and civil causes, of our quarter sessions, and, in a great measure, of our assizes, as courts of nisi prius, of oyer and terminer, and of gaol delivery.

By the law, the district magistrate is obliged to execute much of his duty personally; for instance, when a house robbery (not *theft*) has been reported to him, he must himself examine into the circumstances, repairing to the spot instantly, without regarding " either distance or weather."

Among his other functions, that of coroner of his district is included : for, in cases of violent or unaccountable death, he must personally view the corpse; and if he neglect to do so before putrefaction takes place, he is degraded one step, and removed from his office. If the distance be very great, and he have much business on hand, he may depute a subaltern to hold the inquest; but a punishment hangs over him, if he do so without sufficient cause. If he be absent at the time the event takes place, the subaltern ranking next to him must get the nearest district magistrate, or in case he also be engaged, the nearest superior officer, to undertake the business.

The cases of greater importance must be reported by the district magistrate to the superior mandarins, as they occur, and he must make a monthly report of *all* cases, whether criminal or civil, which are brought before him. Certain periods are fixed by law for the settlement of these cases, and, in fact, for the transaction of every kind of business which it is his duty to

undertake; and a certain penalty is awarded to
the exceeding of each of these periods. He is,
in a great measure, answerable for every thing
that takes place in his district; and is constantly
liable to incur penalties for the faults or crimes
of others, merely for not knowing any thing
about them. If, in that case, the crime or fault
be one involving serious consequences, penalties
are awarded to the superior mandarins, in a sort
of ratio that decreases as the rank of the officers
increases.* If the district magistrate have been
aware of the existence of such criminality, or if
the crime committed be of a very heinous nature,
then these graduated punishments run through
the whole line of superior mandarins to the governor-general himself. In illustration of the
manner in which they are regulated in different
cases, I make the following abstracts from the
" Code of the Board of Civil Office for the punishment of the mandarins."

If, through the neglect of the district magistrate, seditious assemblies are allowed to exist,
until the matter ends in open rebellion, then he
is cashiered; the prefect of the department is
degraded two steps, and removed from his post;
the intendant of the circuit is degraded one step,

* It is of some importance that the agents of foreign governments should keep this fact in view in all their dealings
with the mandarins.

and removed from his post; the judge and the
superintendent of finances are degraded two steps,
but retain their posts (i. e. they are obliged to
assume the button of the first rank next under
them, which, however, as they retain all the
powers and emoluments of their posts, is not a
severe punishment) ; and the governor and the
governor-general are degraded one step, but retain their posts.   In this case none of them are
allowed to balance the account with the extra
" steps " which they usually have in readiness for
such contingencies, and which, in many other
cases, saves them from actual degradation.

If false money have been coined *without* the
knowledge of the district magistrate, he is degraded one step, and removed from his post; and
the prefect of the department is degraded one
step, but retains his post.   If the money have been
coined *with the connivance* of the district magistrate, he is cashiered, and afterwards punished for
the crime as one of the people; while, as it is
one of those which, in a mandarin, is called " private," or " personal," he has little chance of holding office again.   In this latter case, of connivance
on the part of the district magistrate, the prefect,
although ignorant of the matter, or rather, from
being ignorant of it, is degraded two steps, and
removed from his post.

If the sum coined be below ten thousand cash, and above one thousand, and there be no conniv- ance on the part of the authorities, then the dis- trict magistrate is degraded one step, but retains his post; and the prefect is mulcted of one year's salary.*

If the sum coined be below one thousand cash, and there be no connivance on the part of the district magistrate or the prefect, the former is mulcted of one year's salary, and the latter incurs no penalty; on the contrary, if he succeed in bringing the matter to light, and in seizing all the criminals, principals and accessories, he is raised one step.   There are several other distinc- tions made in the matter; and, in short, in all penalties awarded to the mandarins, the distinc- tions in the nature of the crimes and faults, and the consequent modifications of the punishments, are almost interminable.   The forfeit of salary is a penalty so frequently incurred, that the manda- rins seldom or never draw it from the yamun of the superintendent of finances.   If they did, they would be almost certain to have to return it again; and, as in the yamun of such a high functionary, light weights are used in paying, and over-heavy ones in receiving, they would evidently lose by the transaction.

* Not his anti-extortion allowance.   See table of Manda- rins' Titles and Salaries.

11. Hsiên ch ng, assistant district magistrate; chu pu, hsŭn chiên, township magistrate; li mu and tiên shĭ, inspectors of
police; ghŏ pô so, inspectors of river
police.

These officers are subalterns of the district magistrates. The assistant district magistrate has
his yamun generally in a town of the district,
second in size to that of the district city itself;
or in the suburbs of the latter, if they be extensive, as is the case at Canton, where the assistant
district magistrate of Nan Ghai is stationed in
the western suburb, not far from the foreign factories.

Those officers whom, for want of a better term,
I have called township magistrates,* have their
official residences in different parts of the districts
of which their townships form the territorial subdivisions. I cannot describe their duties and
powers, as also those of the assistant district magistrate, better than by saying, that they closely

* These townships contain, on an average, not less than
300 square miles; and it may be remarked here, that the territorial divisions in China are all " en grand." What I call a
township, is a large district; a Chinese district is like a
French department, or an English county; a department is
like a European province; the circuits are like second and
third-rate European kingdoms; and several of the Chinese
provinces rival the first-rate European states, in extent of territory, in wealth, and in population.

resemble those of our justices of the peace when acting singly or at the petit sessions. They have the power of inflicting corporal punishments for a number of minor offences, upon summary conviction, and have large powers of arrest,—either personally, or by issuing a warrant,—vested in them, in cases where they themselves can take no judicial cognizance of the matter. They are sometimes commissioned to examine criminals, and to collect evidence for the district magistrates. In such cases they are not, however, allowed to make use of torture (as beating) to extort evidence or confessions; but must, when that seems necessary, again refer the matter to the personal management of the district magistrate. Notwithstanding this, they themselves, in daily practice, examine by torture in those cases of which they take judicial cognizance on their own authority. The li mu, or the tiĕn shĭ, the inspector of police, always has his yamun in the district city in which, and in so much of the vicinity as is not included in any township, or in the territory of the assistant district magistrate, he exercises the functions of a justice of the peace, acting singly. He has also the more immediate care of the gaols and prisons of the district magistrate; in the discharge of the duties that are thereby incumbent on him, he appears like our visiting justices.

There are only two mandarins in China bearing the title of ghŏ pô so, or inspector of river police, one of whom is stationed in Kwang-tûng, at Canton. His powers and duties resemble those of a justice of the peace when acting singly, but his authority extends only over the population living in boats on the river.

12. CHÎNG LI AND CHAU MÔ, SECRETARIES ; KU TA SHĬ, TREASURER ; SĬ YŬ, PRISON MASTER.

There are twenty-four officers in Kwang-tûng bearing one or other of the above titles, who are placed, three under the superintendent of finances, three under the judge, and the remainder under intendants and prefects. They have all separate establishments, but are nevertheless, in every case, merely the subalterns of the mandarin under whom they are stationed, assisting him in the execution of his *ministerial* duties.

13. GHAI KWAN, SUPERINTENDENT OF CUSTOMS.

His title in Chinese is " superintendent of the maritime customs of Yuê," which latter word is an old name for the country at present included in the provinces of Kwang-tûng and Kwang hši ; but as Kwang hši has no sea-coast, and the word " customs " has, with us, always the idea of mari-time attached to it, he may shortly be entitled, " superintendent of customs for Kwang-tûng."

H

He is frequently called by the more convenient name of "Hoppo," a corruption of ghu pu, the name of "the Board of Revenue," to which he is answerable.

He is not considered by the Chinese as one of the provincial authorities, but I mention him as the one with whom the foreigners have most business to transact. No officer in the province can be promoted to this post, nor can the holder of it receive promotion here. He is always especially deputed from Pekin, and is invariably selected from the Imperial household,* for which reason the Chinese, in speaking of him disparagingly, say, "After all, he is only one of the Emperor's slaves!" The post was formerly the most lucrative one at the disposal of his Imperial Majesty; but as the late treaty with England takes away from the possessor all arbitrary power over the foreign commerce, his income has, in consequence, been very much reduced. However, that part of it derived from the extensive junk trade carried on at various ports in the province, remains undiminished, and there can be little doubt that he will, with the aid, and at the suggestion of his subordinates, very soon have established a safe and lucrative system of smuggling, in connection with the foreign commerce.

As it does not consist with my purpose to give

* Not the Imperial *family*.

any account of the manner in which business is
conducted at the custom-house, I will only refer
those who are desirous of obtaining information
on that subject, to the "Chinese Commercial
Guide," which gives a tolerably correct description of it.

The two last columns of the following table
shew the legal incomes of the mandarins. The
amounts are those given in the "Red Book,"
three taels being reckoned equal to a pound sterling.

I have found it impossible to learn, with any
degree of certainty, what the real incomes of the
mandarins, as increased by illegal fees and special
bribes, may amount to. They vary with the har-
vests, which, according as they are good or bad,
render it easy or difficult to collect the land tax,
—a proceeding in connection with which much
extortion is carried on ; they vary also with the
number of lawsuits, and the wealth of the litigating parties ; and lastly, they vary with the characters of the mandarins and his yemun. The
legal incomes of the lower mandarins are, indeed,
so notoriously insufficient, that they have little
hesitation in speaking, even to a foreigner, of
their other gains, in a general way ; but they
have many reasons for not entering into particulars. Hence, if you do contrive to learn what

H 2

the gross income of any post is on an average, it
is next to impossible to gain any idea of the net
income, i. e. of how much is left after all the
higher mandarins have had their presents, &c.
Under these circumstances, it is little better than
a guess, when I assume the highest mandarins to
get about ten times, the lowest about fifty times,
the amount of their legal incomes. The higher
may get more, but from what individuals of the
lower have said to me, and from what I have
heard and seen of their private outlays, I cannot
think they (the lower) get less. For instance,
one of those, in the receipt of about 22*l.* legal
income, once complained feelingly to me about
his poverty, and on my hinting that his post was,
after all, not a bad one, he protested, with some
earnestness, that his whole income did not exceed
7,000 taels (2,333*l.*), of which he had, he said, to
give a great deal away.   Now this old gentleman
seemed to be one of those who complain on principle, and I am inclined to estimate his *net* income at upwards of 7,000 taels; but his is one of
the best of the lower posts.

A Table exhibiting the Titles, Rank, and Legal Income of the Mandarins.

Official Title in Chinese	Official Title (romanized)	Official Title in English	Title used in direct address in Chinese	Title used in direct address in English	Class	Button	Salary (excepting with the Board) £	Anti-extortion (allowance varying with each Post) £
總督	tsung tu	Governor General	大人 ta jin	Your Excellency	1	Plain & Red	60	8333
巡撫	hsün fu	Governor	ditto	ditto	2	Flowered & Red	60	4333
布政司	pu ching sï	Superintendent of Finances	ditto	ditto	3	ditto	ditto	2606
按察司	an cha sï	Provincial Judge	ditto	ditto	3	Transparent Blue	43	2000
鹽運司	tsaŏ yün sï	Collector of the Salt Gabel	ditto	ditto	3	ditto	ditto	1806
糧儲道	tsang chŭ tao / liang tsü tao	Grain Collector	大老爷 ta lau ye	Your Honor	4	Opaque Blue	35	1966
守巡道	shŏŭ hsün tao / tao tao	Intendant of Circuit	ditto	ditto	4	ditto	ditto	1000 †
知府	chï fu	Prefect of Department	ditto	ditto	4	ditto	ditto	652
直隸州	chï lï chï chŏŭ / chï lï tsing chŏŭ	Prefect of Inferior Department	ditto	ditto	5	Crystal Glass	26	383
同知	t'ŏng chï	Independent Sub-Prefect	ditto	ditto	5	ditto	ditto	340
通判	t'ŏng p'in	Sub-Prefect	ditto	ditto	5	ditto	ditto	295
知州	chï chŏŭ	Deputy Sub-Prefect	ditto	ditto	6	White	20	176
知縣	chï hsien	District Magistrate	ditto	ditto	5	Crystal Glass	26	262
巡檢	hsün ch'ing	ditto	大爷 ta ye	Your Worship	7	Plain Gilt	15	262
州判	chŏŭ pʻi	Assistant District Magistrate	ditto	ditto	8	Gilt with Flowers in relief	15	
巡檢	hsün chien	Township-Magistrate	ditto	ditto	9	Gilt with engraved Flowers	11	
吏目	tʻi mu	Inspector of Police	ditto	ditto	9	ditto	ditto	
典史	tien shï	ditto	ditto	ditto	9	ditto	ditto	
河泊所	ching li	Comptroller of Revenue Police	ditto	ditto	unclassed	ditto	ditto	
經歷 ching ting	ching li	Secretary	ditto	* ditto	6 to 8	From White or Gilt with Flowers in relief / Gilt with Flowers in relief to Gilt with engraved Flowers	20 to 13	
照磨 chaŏ mŏ	chaŏ mŏ	ditto	ditto	ditto	8 to 9	ditto	13 to 18	
庫大使 kʻu ta shï	kʻu ta shï	Treasurer	ditto	ditto	8 to 9	ditto	ditto	
司獄	sï yü	Prison-Master	ditto	ditto	9	Gilt with engraved Flowers	11	
海關	yŭhaï hwan	Superintendent of Customs	大人 ta jin	Your Excellency	3	Transparent Blue	43	833

* The Secretary of the Supt of Finances alone is entitled 大老爷 Your Honor.   † From the Intendant downwards the amount has been taken for the Province.

NOTE IX.

ON THE YAMUN 衙 門 AND THEIR VARIOUS INHABITANTS.

THE yamun are generally called "offices" of the mandarins, in English books and in translations; but as neither this, nor any other word of the English language, gives any thing but a very insufficient idea of the nature of a yamun, I have retained this latter Chinese denomination in these Notes.

I am told that nine-tenths of the numerous yamun in the Chinese empire are built on nearly one and the same plan, and it is certain that they all contain in common four grand divisions; for that we can perceive from the Imperial regulations regarding forms and observances on official visits, which are corroborated by facts incidentally conveyed in the Penal and other codes.

The first, or outermost, of these divisions comprises within it, gaols and places of confinement for short periods; and the dwellings of the chai, or police runners, bailiffs, turnkeys, porters, &c.

The second contains offices (each of which is

frequently composed of several rooms), corresponding to the six supreme boards at Pekin, and some other offices, which vary according to the rank and duties of the mandarin. Only the yamun of the higher mandarins have, however, got an office corresponding to the Board of Civil Office in Pekin; the reason for which is sufficiently obvious, as the business of that Board is to govern mandarins. In these offices of the second division, all the records of the yamun are deposited. The second division contains, also, the great hall, for the formal trial of causes and of criminals, and for other great occasions. It likewise contains the treasury of the yamun.*

The third division includes the office of the mandarin himself, where he superintends the despatch of his correspondence, and of official documents generally, as well as frequently holds judicial examinations; the rooms in which other mandarins, sent by the higher authorities to assist, where the business is great, severally investigate the cases which have been especially handed over to them; the apartments for the reception of visitors, and for giving entertainments; and the

---

* When the yamun of the prefect of Kwang-chôu, in Canton, was taken possession of by the people, in January, 1846, and partially burnt down, this division was left untouched, and the fire-engines allowed to play on it. Chi yîng, the governor-general, was, in consequence, enabled to report to the Emperor, that the money and the records were all safe.

apartments and offices for the shĭ ye and yemun.*
Here is also the kitchen of the mandarin.

This third division is called the nŏi (inner) shu,
in contradistinction to the second, which is called
the wai (outer) shu. The word shu is used very
much like our word office, but with this difference, that it is only employed with reference to
government offices.

The fourth, or innermost division, comprises
the private residence of the mandarin, where the
females of his family and his nearer male relations dwell, and into which no male employed by
him, not even his personal servants, are permitted
to enter. Female domestics only are used here,
and the communication with the kitchen is, in
many yamun, kept up by means of a tub revolv-
ing horizontally in a wall, like the tables used for
a similar purpose in some of the European nun-
neries.

The yamun of a district magistrate, which forms
a very good example of the establishments so
denominated (and is, by the bye, the one most
formidable in the eyes of the people), thus comprises within itself what we would call a general
police station, and the county gaol, as it were,
for the custody of debtors, and of criminals await-
ing trial or execution; the place where courts
equivalent to our quarter sessions and assizes are

* See pages 104 and 107.

held; the offices of all the subordinate officers of these courts; and the office and residence of an official who is at once judge of circuit, sheriff, coroner, and commissioner of taxes. In a populous district it is inhabited by 300 to 500 individuals, and even in thinly inhabited districts, where there is of course less business, it is said to have about 200 inhabitants at least. But the buildings are, it appears, seldom, if ever, so large as this population would lead an Englishman to suppose; for the Chinese can content themselves with an amazingly small extent of space, and these yamun of the district magistrates are generally crowded.

Exclusive of the mandarin and his family, the inhabitants may be divided into four classes.

1. The SHĬ YE 師 爺, the JUDICIAL ADVISERS and PRIVATE SECRETARIES of the mandarin.

These men are the only people in China who devote themselves solely to the study of the law, and, in so far, they resemble our barristers and serjeants-at-law; but they are scarcely ever made mandarins (judges), and none of them act as counsel for either of the litigating parties, in an action at law. Their sole business is to protect the interests of the mandarin, their employer; to point out to him the proper way of conducting his judicial examinations; and to see that the decisions he pronounces are in strict accordance with the laws, and justified by the facts of each particular case, so that he may not incur any of the penalties laid down in the Code of the Board of Civil Office. To obviate this, too, all documents that issue from a yamun, are revised by these men, and those of importance are drafted by them. Although their existence is well known to all Chinese, they are not recognized by government as official servants, but are in the private employ of the mandarins. For this reason, they are never personally present at judicial examinations; though the course of these latter are, as stated above, in a great measure regulated by their opinions.

The most important of the shǐ ye are the hsîng mîng (punishment list) shǐ ye, who confine their attention to the criminal law. Next to them stand the chiên ku (money and grain, i. e. revenue) shǐ ye, who apply themselves chiefly to the fiscal laws. Besides these two classes, which properly comprise the *judicial advisers*, there are shu pin (write report) shǐ ye, whose business it is to take charge of the half-official correspondence of the mandarin with his superiors; and kwan chang (manage accounts) shǐ ye, who superintend the keeping of the official accounts. These, and some similar classes of shǐ ye, may very well be denominated *private secretaries*. Each yamun has generally one shǐ ye of each class: but when

the business is very great, there are two hsîng
mîng shǐ ye.

The hsîng mîng, or criminal law, shǐ ye, of district magistrates of populous districts, get fixed
salaries of about 2,000 dollars per annum, paid
by their employers.   The fixed salaries of those
in the higher yamun do not much exceed this
sum ; but, in addition to it, they get annual presents from the mandarins subject to the authority
of the one whom they serve.   If any subordinate
mandarin were to refuse this tribute, every appeal
to a superior tribunal would involve him in trouble.   The amount of these presents is said to be
1,000 or 2,000 dollars per annum, according to
the number of subordinate mandarins ; but it is
necessary to warn the reader here, that there are
few things connected with China about which it
is more difficult to obtain correct information,
than the real incomes of people employed in the
transaction of official business, whether such people be recognized by government, or otherwise.

All the shǐ ye increase their incomes by taking
pupils, with whom they receive an entrance fee of
a few hundred dollars ; and who, as they grow
up, assist them in the transaction of official business.   When a safe opportunity offers, too, they
" open the back door," as the Chinese call it, i. e.
take bribes ; but the nature of their business,
viz. the interpretation and application of the law.

generally in grave cases, and which is subse-
quently recorded, does not permit much of this.
For this reason, and because it requires a long
pupilage and hard study to make a hsîng mîng
shĭ ye, he gets a larger *fixed* salary than perhaps
any other Chinese in private employ.

The income of the chiên ku, or fiscal law, shĭ
ye, is about one half of that of the hsîng mîng shĭ
ye. The others, whom I have called *private
secretaries*, get, even where best paid, only from
200 to 500 dollars per annum.

The shĭ ye are a respectable class of men in
the eyes of the Chinese; and it in no wise dero-
gates from the dignity of the mandarin, their employer, to invite them to his table, and associate
with them on terms of intimacy.

2. The YEMUN 爺 們, the FOLLOWERS of the
mandarin.

We have in England nothing similar to this
class of men; and very fortunately so, for the
chief of them are the negotiators of all the special bribes, and the channels through which the
other illegal gains of a mandarin are conveyed to
his purse.

They are, like the shĭ ye, in the private employ
of the mandarin, but they get no fixed pay, being
remunerated solely by a portion of the bribes,
&c. that pass through their hands. The lower of
them are the personal attendants of the manda-

rin, but the higher, who have the distinctive title of 門 上 mun shang (upon the gate), never perform any menial offices.* To each of these higher followers, the mandarin, as soon as he enters upon his office, assigns a particular duty. This will be deputed to receive the bribes from the gambling houses and other illegal establishments connived at by the mandarin in different parts of the territory subject to his jurisdiction; one will have the custody and superintend the use of the official seal,† and so on. The most important among them, and, next to the mandarin, the most influential man in the yamun, is the *kau an* (draft case) *mun shang*. The business of this man is to report to the mandarin all applications made at the yamun, or any thing that may have occurred requiring his attention; and then to see that the proper persons set about the execution of such measures as the mandarin may see fit to adopt; to settle the amount of all the

* They have, on the contrary, their own servants, who are called *san ye*, i. e. *third ye*, a phrase that is something like what " gentleman's gentleman's gentleman " would be in English; for their masters, in addition to the term mun shang, are also called *u̐ ye*, i. e. *second ye*, and ye gives most of the compounds in which it occurs the signification of the German Herr, i. e. gentleman, Mr., Master, or lord, as the case may be.

† In the higher yamun, as those of the governor-general, the governor, and superintendent of finances, mandarins are appointed to take this charge.

extraordinary or *special** bribes to be demanded
from the different parties in lawsuits, according to
their ability to pay, and the urgency of the causes
that oblige them to pay ; and to receive presents
from mandarins subject to his master, and trans-
mit those from his master to higher ones.

In the temporary absence of the mandarin, the
kau an mun shang will, after consulting with the
shĭ ye, order preliminary steps to be taken in any
urgent case that may suddenly occur. He is
often a relation of the mandarin, and not unfrequently the person who advanced him funds
wherewith to bribe his way into his post, and
who then accompanies him to it, in order to get
repaid. It is evident the mandarin can place
implicit confidence in his zeal, if he belong to this
latter class, since his only chance of being repaid
depends on the mandarin's retaining his place.
Many of the mun shang are persons recommended
by higher mandarins to their present masters, and
the number of such persons recommended to a
new mandarin is often so great, as to cause him
much embarrassment, from his inability to employ
them.

A mandarin will also sometimes promote a clever personal attendant, who has been long in his
service, to the post of a mun shang, and even to

* These are exclusive of a number of illegal, but tolerably
well ascertained fees, exacted by the shu pan and chai yŭ.

that of kau an mun shang. However they may
have got their places, they are, notwithstanding
the great influence they exercise, always considered as domestics, and are frequently called chia
jĕn, household people. They are, therefore, not
looked on as fit associates for the mandarins, and
cannot presume to sit in the presence of their
own master. The lower mandarins are, however,
glad to keep on good terms with the mun shang
of their superiors; and I have seen crystal and
white button mandarins very profuse in their
civilities to the kau an mun shang of the governor-general.

It is quite impossible to say what the annual
income of these people may be, as it varies so
much in different yamun, and in the same yamun
at different times, depending, in a great measure,
on the number and wealth of litigants; but I
may mention, that the Chinese frequently speak
of the more fortunate of the kau an mun shang
getting so much as ten, twenty, and thirty thousand taels in a single year. Others, again, do not
get more than a few hundred taels annually.

The persons who examine goods on the part of
the custom-house at Canton, are mun shang of
the superintendent of customs, or hoppo (to whose
yamun, by the bye, the remarks in this Note do
not apply, it containing no court of law); and
there is generally a yemun of his in charge of

each of the numerous customs' stations on the river.

3. The SHU PAN 書 辨. These are CLERKS recognized by government, frequent mention being made of them by the Penal and other codes. According to law, they ought to be changed every five years; it being apprehended that if they retained their places for a longer period, *they would become so intimately acquainted with the business of the yamuns, as to be able to commit malpractices;* but the post of shu pan has, in the higher yamun of Kwang-tûng, and, I am told, of the other provinces also, become virtually the property of the holders, who can let or sell it altogether, during their lifetime, and leave it to their children at their death. So long as they themselves retain it, they are, however, obliged to change their names at the end of every five years. The mandarin who connives at this proceeding is, indeed, to be cashiered, and if it be done without his knowledge, he is to be degraded two steps, and removed from his post; yet the practice is well known to be quite common, and this, therefore, forms one of the many instances in which the provisions of the Chinese laws stand in direct contradiction to the actual practice. Here, too, as in many other instances, the low standard at which the salaries of the mandarins are fixed, is the ultimate cause of the evil; I say

evil, for such a too intimate acquaintance, on the part of the government agent, with the affairs of the country where he is placed, really proves itself to be, in China, under the present state of things.

The business of the shu pan is to take charge of the records, to keep accounts connected with the revenue, to make out fair copies of documents issued from the yamun, and to draft those of less importance. Where secrecy is required, though, they are not allowed to see official papers until the affairs to which they relate have been settled. Among papers of this sort, I may instance, letters of any importance concerning the various tribes that maintain themselves in a semi-independent state, in different mountain ranges of the mainland, and on the islands of Formosa and Ghainan; and although the laws, as yet printed, do not seem to have provided for such a contingency as official correspondence with " barbarians " from the sea, I have no doubt, that a very great part of that now carried on does not find its way into the outer offices. If a mandarin gives letters of importance, concerning mountaineers of the interior, to the shu pan, to be copied, he is to be degraded one step, but to retain his post; and his immediate superior is to be mulcted of six months' salary.

The yamun of the district magistrate of a populous district contains about one hundred shu pan, who work in ten or fifteen offices, situated in the second division of the establishment.

The shu pan have an allowance from government of one or two taels per month; but their incomes are chiefly derived from the illegal, but well ascertained, fees of office, which all litigants and other applicants at the yamun must pay, and which are shared in certain fixed proportions. These are, in some yamun, so great, as to render a shu-pan-ship a respectable property for a man of the middle classes.

In the seventh month of every year, those shu pan who have served for five years, and who desire it, are, after presenting certificates from the mandarin under whom they served, examined by the governor-general and the governor, or by their special deputies; and a report is sent in to the central government, which then confers one of the lowest ranks on those recommended, and also employs some of them as township magistrates and police magistrates. Those, however, who are promoted to these inferior magistracies, have mostly served in one of the higher yamun at Pekin.

4. The CHAI YŬ 差 役. This is a general designation for the police, thief-takers, bailiffs, and turnkeys of China. As the duties of these classes of public servants are sufficiently well known, it is needless to enumerate them.

The chai yŭ are, like the shu pan, recognized
by the general government, and a trifling monthly
pay is allotted to them; but they derive their
support from the illegal fees of the yamun, from
bribes for permitting delays when entrusted with
a warrant for the apprehension of any one, &c.
&c.   In addition to this, many of the head men
among them are in connection with gangs of robbers, who pay for their connivance and protection.   They are the instruments by which all extortions are ultimately effected; and are used
frequently by the mun shang, as middlemen, to
do the higgling, when he is negotiating for special bribes.   As in the case of the shu pan, their
places in the higher yamun are their property,
which they let and sell, in defiance of all the
prohibitions of the laws.

———————

From what is above stated in this Note, the
reader will have concluded, that the interior of a
busy yamun must present a very bustling scene.
The yamun of a district magistrate is, from the
nature and multiplicity of the functions of this
mandarin, the most busy of any; and the two
which are situated in Canton, viz. the district
yamun of Nan ghai, and that of Pan yŭ, where a
number of criminal cases from other districts of
the provinces are investigated by mandarins spe-

cially deputed for that purpose,* form, I am told,†
a very striking spectacle, from the great stir that
pervades them from sunrise to sunset. The almost
unceasing flail-like sounds of beating with the
bamboo, either as a punishment for ascertained
guilt, or to extort confessions and evidence; the
cries of the sufferers; the voices of the examining
mandarins questioning, bullying, and wheedling;
the voices of the porters stationed at the doors
between the first and second, and the second and
third divisions, transmitting, in a loud singing
tone, orders for shu pan of different offices and
chai yǔ of various sorts to repair to certain places
in the yamun where they are wanted; the constant running hither and thither of some of the
latter personages and of the other inhabitants of
the place; and the frequent appearance of criminals and witnesses being escorted to and from the
prisons and rooms for examination, are sounds
and sights that bewilder and agitate those who
have not been accustomed to them, and serve to
heighten that dread which all private Chinese
entertain of entering a yamun.

Such, at least, is the idea the descriptions of

* The district magistrates constantly keep a table for the
mandarins so deputed, at which they are, however, not expected to appear themselves, since that would preclude their
even taking a meal in private.

† Our exclusion from the city of Canton has prevented me
from seeing the places myself.

the Chinese, joined to circumstances incidentally mentioned, would lead me to form of the interior of the two yamun above named ; but the reader must remember that these are the busiest establishments of this sort in the second city of the empire

NOTE X.

ON THE TI PAU 地 保 AND THE TAI SHU 代 書.

The ti pau is a person whose powers and duties resemble those of our constables, but with this difference, this his power (by law) is not so great as that of an English constable, and he has a responsibility lying on him which is not incumbent on the latter.

In cities, his authority and responsibility extend to a few streets; in the country, to the quarter or whole of a town or village, according to their size, and including sometimes a portion of the open country in the neighbourhood to the distance of a few miles.

One of his chief duties is to make himself acquainted with the names and occupations of the inhabitants of his quarter, so that when any of them have occasion to apply to the courts of law, i. e. to the yamun, he may be able to certify that the applicants are the people they state themselves to be. For this purpose, a wooden seal or stamp is given to him, and no petitions or accusations are received at the yamun unless a ti pau's seal is affixed to them. When a warrant

or summons is issued, the police runner to whom
it is entrusted always applies in the first place to
the ti pau within whose quarter the person to be
summoned or apprehended is said to live, and it
is then the duty of the ti pau to accompany him
in order to point out the person; but he is never
called on to serve a summons or execute a warrant himself. He can, however, arrest without
warrant in all cases where a crime or misde-
meanor is committed in his presence.

In less serious cases of theft in the streets, it
is incumbent on the ti pau both to search out the
thief and also recover the stolen property; and if
he fail to do so within a certain time fixed by the
magistrate, the latter orders a certain number of
blows with the bamboo to be inflicted on him.
Another period is then fixed, at the expiration
of which he is again beaten if he have not succeeded; and he is sometimes subjected to several
of these punishments. For this reason, the ti
pau, particularly those in large cities, take care
to be well acquainted with all thieves by profession, who, it is said, share their spoils with them,
and thus secure immunity in such cases as are not
brought by the sufferers to the notice of the
magistrate. But when this latter takes up any
case seriously, the ti pau, as a matter of course,
sacrifices his friends. This connection of the ti
pau with the thieves accounts for their being

able to recover stolen property to a degree that would otherwise be quite astonishing.

In grave cases of robbery or murder, he is not held responsible for the discovery of the criminals, but he must report the cases as soon as they occur to the mandarins. Should it, however, be proved that a ti pau was aware of the existence of felons, as such, in his quarter, he is liable to punishment.

He is, in short, the chief *informing officer* of the quarter to which his authority extends, being bound to inform against all criminals and suspicious persons; as, for instance, against travellers who pass the night in his quarter, having with them children apparently kidnapped, &c. &c.

He hires the watchmen and people who keep guard at the gates, to be seen at the end of every Chinese street, and which are regularly closed at night.

Exclusive of the presents from thieves, noticed above, his emoluments consist of donations made at certain periods of the year by the householders of his quarter, and fees paid him on affixing his stamp to petitions. In cities, too, he derives no small profit from the gambling houses, the existence of which he connives at in common with the people of the yamun.

When the post of a ti pau becomes vacant, either

from death or superannuation, the householders of the quarter meet in a temple to select a person to fill the vacancy. Previously, they generally post notices that a ti pau is wanted for such and such a locality, and that candidates must offer themselves at the election, which is to take place on a certain specified day. As is usual, whenever large assemblies have the decision, the selection is made virtually beforehand, by a few of the more influential. To these influential individuals, therefore, the candidates apply first.

After a person has been selected, the householders send in a report, signed by all, to the magistrate within whose immediate jurisdiction the place lies, i. e. to the township magistrate if it be in the country, and the district magistrate if it be in a city. The magistrate invariably confirms the selection, and formally delivers over to the new ti pau the chiô, the wooden seal or stamp held by his predecessor.

The station of a ti pau in society is below that of a respectable tradesman or a master mechanic, though his influence be more generally felt.

The pai tôu, and the chia tôu, whose establishment, the former over every ten families, the latter over every hundred families, is provided for in the Penal Code, chapter 20, section 5, clause 3, do not now seem to exist except in that work ;*

* As far as regards Kwang-tûng at least. The institu-

but the ti pau seems to have originally been the pau chang or overseer of one thousand families, mentioned in the clause just referred to. At all events he is now found in all parts of China, his title appearing frequently in the Pekin Gazette, in connection with cases reported from all the different provinces, and it has existed for a long time back.

The tai shu are half official personages somewhat resembling our attorneys, their business being the same in its nature. But it would seem that they are not recognized by the general government; and it is certain that in looking over the Chinese codes I have never seen them noticed. The great convenience, nay, the absolute necessity where there is much business, of having attached to courts of law some persons to act for litigants acquainted with the forms of business, and able to free documents intended to be presented there from irrelevant matter, has, however, been the cause of the establishment in practice of the tai shu ; and as each mandarin on assuming office holds an examination of persons desirous of acting in this capacity at his yamun, they may be said to have been formally admitted by the courts at which they practise.

tion of pai tôu and chia tôu resembles that of headborough and high constable of King Alfred the Great.

After the examination just alluded to, the mandarin gives into the custody of such as he may select, the wooden stamps held by the tai shu, and which are delivered every time the mandarinship becomes vacant. Usually the same individuals who acted in this capacity before, are again selected, but this is not always the case; hence an insecurity of the post, which, joined to the circumstance of its not being recognized by the general government, renders the calling a comparatively much less respectable one, than the profession of attorney in England.

The tai shu pastes up a large red card (equivalent to our brass plates) at his door, stating his occupation, and the name of the yamun at which he practises. He generally lives in the neighbourhood of the latter. His business, strictly speaking, is confined to the putting into a proper form his client's accusation or defence; which he generally demands from him in writing, and retains as a proof that he himself has not made additions to the statements contained in it. It is said, however, that the tai shu sometimes invent stories for their clients when their cases are not strong, and also give them such advice, as " You should contrive to provoke your opponent to give you a beating, &c. &c." If it comes out, though, that they have done this, the mandarin will order their stamps to be taken from them.

Their incomes are derived from fees paid by their clients for the documents they prepare, or for affixing an impression of their stamp to such as are presented to them ready drawn up; for without an impression of a tai shu's stamp, no accusations or petitions are formally received at the yamun. The tai shu hand in the papers of their clients to the yamun, and disburse for them the various customary but illegal fees.

NOTE XI.

ON THE CAUSE OF THE LONG DURATION OF THE CHINESE EMPIRE.

THE long duration of the Chinese empire is solely and altogether owing to the operation of a principle, which the policy of every successive dynasty has practically maintained in a greater or less degree, viz. *that good government consists in the advancement of men of talent and merit only, to the rank and power conferred by official posts.*

The existence of a system of examinations, based on this principle, is well known to every educated European; and it is literally impossible to conceive that the various writers on China, from the Jesuit missionaries who lived upwards of 150 years ago, to the sinologues of the present day, can have failed to perceive the effects of this institution;—effects so obvious, and so distinctly pointed out by Chinese writers, as to require no penetration to discover them. Yet, strange to say, all those whose works I have been enabled to peruse seem to attribute the long duration and stability of the Chinese empire, chiefly to

the influence of the doctrine of filial piety, as inculcated by the Chinese sages.* Now this doctrine,
I maintain, does nothing as a *fundamental* cause

* " The vital and universally operating principle of the
Chinese government is the duty of submission to parental
authority, whether vested in the parents themselves or in
their representatives ; and which, although usually described
under the pleasing appellation of filial piety, is much more
properly to be considered as a general rule of action than as
the expression of any particular sentiment of affection. It
may easily be traced even in the earliest of their records ; it
is inculcated with the greatest force in the writings of the
first of their philosophers and legislators ; it has survived each
successive dynasty, and all the various changes and revolutions
which the state has undergone ; and it continues to this day
powerfully enforced, both by positive laws and by public
opinion.

" A government, constituted upon the basis of parental authority, thus highly estimated and extensively applied, has certainly the advantage of being directly sanctioned by the
immutable and ever-operating laws of nature, and must
thereby acquire a degree of firmness and durability to which
governments, founded on the fortuitous superiority of particular individuals, either in strength or abilities, and continued
only through the hereditary influence of particular families, can
never be expected to attain. Parental authority and preroga-
tive seem to be obviously the most respectable of titles, and
parental regard and affection the most amiable of characters,
with which sovereign or magisterial power can be invested,
and are those under which, it is natural to suppose, it may
most easily be perpetuated.

" By such principles, the Chinese have been distinguished
ever since their first existence as a nation ; by such ties, the
vast and increasing population of China is still united as one
people, subject to one supreme government, and uniform in

to uphold the unity and stability of the Chinese
empire; its influence, great though it undoubtedly
be, could not of itself resist the existing causes of
dismemberment for a single generation; and
even for that influence, for all that is peculiar in
the practical hold it possesses on the minds of
the Chinese people, it is indebted to the principle
referred to above, as the sole cause of the long
duration of the empire.

Against so many high authorities, however,
mere assertions will have little weight; I, therefore, subjoin some remarks, which it is hoped
will leave no doubt on the mind of the reader
in connection with this subject.

I first proceed to show by extracts from the
Chinese classics, their most ancient works, that
the principle to which I have referred, was recognized by the Chinese government many centuries before the Christian era; and by extracts
from papers of writers, who either sat on the
throne, or held high government posts since the
days of Confucius and his disciples; that it has,
during the succeeding periods, been constantly
more or less acted upon, *and moreover, looked upon*

its habits, manners, and language.   In this state, in spite of
every internal and external convulsion, it may possibly very
long continue."   (Staunton's Preface to his translation of the
" Penal Code.")

by them as forming in its operation the principal support of government.*

The following was said in a conversation which took place between the Emperor Shun and his successor Yu. Yu commenced to reign B.C 2205.

"When a king, says Yu, knows how difficult it is to be a good king, and when a subject knows how much it costs to fulfil all his duties faithfully, the government is perfect, and the people make a swift progress in the ways of virtue. That is certain, replied the Emperor; and I love to be discoursed with in this manner. Truths so well grounded, ought never to be concealed. Let all wise men be distinguished, and not one of them suffered to remain in oblivion; then all the kingdoms of the world will enjoy a profound peace. But to rest entirely upon the sentiments of wise men,—to prefer them to his own; to treat orphans with kindness; and never to reject the suit of the poor, are perfections only to be found in a very wise king."

The following was addressed to the Emperor Ching tang, who commenced to reign B.C. 1783.

* The extracts are all taken from translations contained in Du Halde, or from Collie's translation of the Four Books. Those from the latter work have in most instances been compared with the original; but I have not been able to obtain the originals of the papers translated in Du Halde. The dates I have taken from original Chinese chronologies.

He was the founder of a dynasty, and the
Keĕ alluded to was the last of the house of
Hea.

"You know that the cruel Keĕ had likewise
some wise men about his person, but most of his
counsellors were as worthless as himself..........
You are looked upon as a very wise prince, and
far removed from all base pleasures, as being entirely disinterested, bestowing posts only upon the
virtuous, and always proportioning the reward to
the merit..........One must have no scruple to
be a king, but he must labour to render himself
a good king.*   With this view distinguish the
wise and assist the worthy."

The following was addressed to the successor
of Ching tang, Tae kea, who commenced to reign
B.C. 1753.

"Heir of Ching tang! the empire you possess
is but new; let your virtue be new likewise.
Endeavour, by incessantly reforming yourself,
that there may be no difference between the first
and the last day of your reign.   Raise none to
posts, but such as have wisdom and talents.   But
as for your first minister, he ought to be a person
accomplished in all respects."

The Emperor Woo ting, who commenced to
reign B.C. 1324, after having sent over the whole

* Ching tang was almost forced by the nation to dethrone
Keĕ, and reign in his stead.

empire to find a good minister, at last found one, who, in the conversation that took place between them, gave him the following advice :—

"Shame can only come to kings by their issuing forth unjust orders : and the rebellions of the people only proceed from their princes making war upon too slight grounds. Bestow no reward but upon merit. Clothes had better be locked up in a chest, than given away without any reason. Before you punish any one, examine yourself well. A king who perfectly fulfils these four points is truly enlightened, and every thing conspires to render him happy. The repose or the distraction of your empire depends upon those whom you place in posts. Give not, therefore, the smallest employments away in complaisance to a subject, whom you know is incapable to bear it ; and never trust any thing of importance to a bad man, however great his qualifications may be."

The following are the opinions and injunctions of Confucius on this subject, as recorded in the Four Books. He was born B. C. 551.

" Good government depends on obtaining proper men.........Justice is what is right in the nature of things ; its highest exercise is to honour men of virtue and talents."

" Gae Kung asked how he might secure the submission of the people ? Confucius replied,

Promote the upright, and put down the vicious, and the people will obey."*

" Chung kung, when first minister to Ke she, asked respecting government. Confucius said, In the first place, have suitable officers under you; pardon small offences; and promote men of virtue and talents."

"Confucius said, Chwang wăn chung was a secret robber of office. He knew that Lew-Hea-Hwuy was a man of eminent talents and virtue, and yet did not promote him to a place equal to his own."

The following are the opinions of Mencius, also recorded in the Four Books. He is mentioned in the chronology as having gone from his native principality, Tsoo, to that of Wei, B. C. 336.

" Mencius says, The virtuous have glory, the vicious disgrace. To hate disgrace, and yet practise vice, is like hating dampness, and yet dwelling in a low room. If a prince hate it (disgrace), then, there is nothing he can do better than to honour virtue and respect the learned."

" When the virtuous occupy official stations, and men of talents are in office, then, when the

---

* In perusing these extracts, the reader would do well to remember the following passage :—

Wie soll ich eine so lang bewährte Ueberzeugung aufgeben, daß Geist und Talent bei keinem verderbten Herzen wohnen? . . . . Ist es möglich? Ich begreife es nicht — So gesunde Begriffe, so viel Geist bei einem so weggeworfenen Character.—(Schiller's Parasit.)

members of government have leisure, they will illustrate the laws, so that even an extensive country will fear and respect them."

Speaking of celebrated Emperors of former times, he says, " When they entered a province, if the lands were well cultivated and the fields in good order—the aged nourished, superiors respected, and men of virtue and talents in official situations—they rewarded the princes by a grant of land."

" Mencius says, When men of virtue and talents are not confided in, the country is empty (of men)."

The above extracts are all taken from old works, that to this day constitute to a Chinese the highest authorities ; the following will serve to show what practical influence they have had in a succession of subsequent ages.

The Emperor Wan te, who ascended the throne B.C. 179, published a declaration in which he says :—

" The great Yu was at extraordinary pains to procure virtuous and able persons to assist him in governing wisely. The orders he published for this effect were not only published within the bounds of the empire, but were known a great way beyond them ; and we may say, they were unknown only to countries inaccessible to ships, to chariots, and to men. Every one, both far and near, esteemed it both a pleasure and a duty to communicate to him their knowledge; by these means, this great prince was never seen to take one wrong step, and became the founder of a long and flourishing dynasty. Kaou te, in later times, has taken the same precautions in founding our dynasty. After he had delivered the empire from its calamities, his first care was, as much as he could, to furnish himself with men of merit. All such he put in posts, and recommended nothing so strongly to them, as to help him to govern aright. Aided by the powerful protection of providence (teen), and the fortune of his family, and peaceably possessing his large kingdom, he extended the effects of his goodness even to neighbouring people. From him, you know it, the empire devolves on me. You know, likewise (for I have often told you so myself), that I have neither virtue nor qualifications sufficient for the weight of government. This engages me to publish the present declaration, to enjoin all who are in posts in my empire, from the prince to the simple magistrate, to enquire carefully after persons of merit for my service. Such, for instance, as know the world perfectly well; others who have a thorough understanding of all affairs relating to the state; but above all, such as have resolution and honesty enough to inform me freely of what they think amiss in my conduct. '

The Emperor Tae tsung, of the Tang dynasty, who ascended the throne A.D. 627, after commenting on the cause of the ruin of several former dynasties, and attributing it to the blindness of the Emperors, "both to their duties and to their defects," goes on to say, "It is in order to shun this blindness, that after having seen, by reading history, what are the principles of good government, and what are the springs of commotions, of all these I compose a mirror for myself, in which I may behold my faults, in order to endeavour to amend them. The most essential character of good government is, not to raise any to posts but men of merit and virtue. A prince who acts thus reigns happily; but there is nothing more dangerous and fatal for a state than a contrary conduct. Is a prince in any difficulty? He never fails to consult his ministers, and his other great officers. If these are all understanding, zealous men, let the danger be ever so great, it seldom ends in his losing all."

The following was addressed by Loo ke to the Emperor Tih tsung, who ascended the throne A.D. 780.

" In short, to desire to govern well, and not to make it your principal study to gain the hearts of your subjects, is pursuing wrong measures: without this, never did any prince succeed. But what measures must be pursued, in order to gain

the hearts of the subjects? You must study to
court and search for men of merit; you must
even make advances to them, in order to bring
them over to your service. I say you must *court
and search for men of merit;* for if a prince acts
in the same manner with all the world indifferently, men of merit will not come near him at
all. Nothing then is more important for a prince,
than justly to distinguish true merit."

In a paper drawn up by the same Loo ke for
the same Emperor Tih tsung, the latter is made to
say: " The first principle of a wise government
is, to honour virtue; earnestly to search for men
of virtue and merit, is the chief duty of a prince :
These are maxims universally received in all ages."

The following was addressed by Sze ma kwang
to the Emperor Ying tsung, who ascended the
throne A.D. 1064.

" It is a common and a true saying, that in
point of personal perfection, filial piety is the chief
of all virtues, and equity is the soul of government."

After discussing the first point, he reasons at
considerable length to demonstrate the second
proposition. The following are some extracts :—

" The great rule of sovereigns is, to reward virtue, and to punish vice; to advance men of probity
and merit, and to banish all who want both.
Honours and posts, being the most precious trea-

sures of states, a prince ought not to distribute
them to his subjects whose only merit is, that
they agree with him in some particular notions."
*   *   *   *   *   *
" At present, there is a great mixture among the
officers of your empire.   There are amongst them
men of virtue and merit, but they are mixed and
confounded in the crowd.   The good and the bad
are upon a footing.   This is a disorder infinitely
prejudicial to the good of the state, and I would
wish that your majesty would seriously apply to
remedy it.   The thing you must do for that effect,
is as follows: Lay yourself out to know those
thoroughly, whose virtue and capacity are greater
than ordinary, and who are thereby most capable
to answer the hopes of the public.   Such as you
know to be men of this kind, draw immediately
out of the crowd, advancing them to the first
posts ; and though they had formerly the unhap-
piness to displease you, yet do not fail to promote
them in proportion to their services.   Act in the
same manner with regard to punishments.   *   *
*   *   *   But, on the contrary, if your
majesty, leading an idle life in your palace, and
abandoning yourself to your pleasures, should
devolve your authority on some one of your officers ; if, without examining who has, or who has
not, merit ; without distinguishing genuine virtue
from vice artfully disguised ; or regarding any

consequences, you put all indifferently into posts;
the first who shall present: or, which is worse
still, if making your inclinations or your resent-
ments your rule, if you banish from you all those
who have formerly displeased you, and advance
only those whom you have always favoured; if
you use the power of rewarding, only that you
may gratify sycophants who have no merit, and
who have done no service, and that of punishing,
only that you may check zealous loyal subjects,
whose uprightness is all their crime; then every
thing will soon rush to confusion, both at court
and in the provinces: there will be no more
law, no more order, no more peace. Can any
thing be more fatal both to the empire in general,
and to your majesty in particular? These are the
reasons why I said that equity is the principal point
of government, in the same manner as in personal
perfection filial piety is the first of all virtues."

Sze ma kwang, the writer of the above, was
no obscure scholar, envious of those in the possession of posts from which he found himself
excluded. He held a high post under the Emperor Jin tsung, the immediate predecessor of
Ying tsung; under which latter sovereign, in
the fourth year of his reign, he was created a
member of the Han lin college, and four years
after, in the next following reign, he was made
assistant minister. He was well acquainted with

former times, having written one of the best his-
torical works extant, and as he is still looked
back to by the whole nation as a statesman of
the first order, he may be considered a conclusive
authority. Now, in the above paper, he distinctly
places filial piety and strict equity in the conduct
of the sovereign towards the people in juxtaposi-
tion; to the first he attributes good personal and
domestic effects, which in China certainly do
result from it; but it is the latter alone which he
makes to consist entirely in rewarding virtue and
promoting talent, in punishing vice and degrading
incapacity, that he esteems the basis and main-
spring of good government.

Upwards of three centuries before the time of
Sze ma kwang, a system of examinations was
established, with the sole view of gaining the
talent of the country for the service of government. In A.D. 736, the vice-presidents of the
Board of Rites received orders to make these
examinations the object of their especial care;
and the system has been gradually extended as
well as improved in its organization, up to the
present moment, when, as I have frequently
occasion to observe, a literary graduate, though
poor, is much more respected, and really possesses
a greater practical influence, than the rich but
unlearned merchant or landed proprietor.

Having now, as I think, fairly proved that the

principle alluded to has from the earliest times
been practically applied in China, and actually
considered by those best able to judge, as of vital
importance to the existence of the empire, I shall
endeavour to show in what manner the application
of this principle operates, to produce the effects
ascribed to it.

First then, *the strict equity of the principle*
makes the untalented submit cheerfully to whatever
is founded on it ; and as a CERTAIN *path is open to*
every man of real talent, able demagogues are rare.

However much the heart of man may be originally inclined to evil, it will scarcely be denied
that strict equity is somehow very congenial to his
feelings, and even though he may himself be a suf-
ferer by it, there is something in it that silences
him the moment it is fully recognized as equity by
his own mind. Now that kind of equity which
consists in elevating the truly meritorious, is
peculiarly pleasing to human beings, so much so,
that they will endure from a person so elevated,
much that would, coming from another, be resisted
to the utmost of their power. In addition to
this, even such persons as have been, from poverty
or other circumstances, unable to procure an
education, or whose want of capacity prevents
them from acquiring knowledge, even these are
interested in the impartial advancement of talent.
If they be fathers, then their sons are making great

progress at school, and will one day, it is hoped, raise themselves to high rank ; if they be childless, then they have brothers or some near relations, who either have attained or are rapidly advancing towards an honourable station. Moreover, in a country where, as in China, this principle has been so long acted upon, nearly every man has had an ancestor in a post of greater or less rank, and whose honourable reputation in some measure descends to him. The practical application of this principle is, in fact, that "stake in the hedge" for all orders, which political economists esteem so much, as interesting the people in the preservation of the public tranquillity, and inspiring them with an attachment to their country and its institutions.

As to the second part of the proposition, I quote in illustration the following extracts from an address to the throne of the Chinese statesman, Soo shih, who was made minister in the first year of the reign of Che tsung, A.D. 1068.

" One of the things which our ancient kings feared most, was, lest some of their subjects, losing courage, and despairing of success, should entirely abandon the care of his honour and fortune. These wise princes well knew that when it comes to that pass, they never stop half way in wickedness, but hold on till they commonly become incorrigible. For which reason, one of

their greatest cares was to act in such a manner
as that their subjects, being always animated by
fear and hope, should never be weary of doing good.
With this view, having established different de-
grees of distinction, and different posts, to which
considerable appointments were annexed, they
never bestowed them but upon deserving persons;
but they never laid any man under an incapacity
of enjoying them, and thereby, they animated
every one to aspire to them. The road to these
posts and honours was open to all their subjects ;
and they who did not arrive at them, could not
justly impute it to any thing but their own dis-
orders and weakness.   Thus there was seen
through all the orders of the state, not only a
great ardour for well doing, but likewise an
admirable constancy not to relax nor prevaricate."

   " But still what secret had our ancient princes
to arrive at this ?   It was as follows : being per-
suaded that the son of a man of quality, when he
degenerates, has nothing that can in reason set
him above the level of the most common people,
they had regard to nothing but to merit and
capacity ; they were so determined in this, that be
his birth what it would, without these two qualifications, he never could propose to be advanced.
Thereby, men of a high birth had a check put
upon that licentiousness which is so natural to
them, and they endeavour to support their rank ;

thereby, the meanest who were conscious of virtue had a spur to excite them ; thereby, throughout all the empire a generous emulation, which produced admirable effects, increased every day. O ! what just notions had these ancient princes !................What I think still worse is, that those of a certain condition are either entirely precluded, or some bounds are assigned them, beyond which they cannot pass. The officers of the Chow and the Heen, when they are once divested of their posts, can never recover them. These then become people who, being reduced to despair, and who, having nothing further to hope for or to fear, grow capable of any thing, and do great mischief among the people. Such a one amongst them at the bottom is an honest man; he has merit and capacity; an unlucky accident happens to him, for which he is broken.* Thenceforward no more employments to him, he is put under an everlasting incapacity, and is a man who, contrary to the maxims of our ancients, is rendered desperate, and who consequently is exposed to the temptation of being very wicked."

That the well directed and energetic exertions

* See the Note on " The Principal Defects of the Chinese Government," in which I have endeavoured to shew that the system of punishing mandarins for " accidents " is bad in the extreme.

of men that *will* rise in one way or the other, by
the unassisted powers of their own minds, have,
among the nations of the west, been productive
of the most beneficial, or the most ruinous effects,
according as the governments under which such
men existed, have made them friends or enemies,
is a fact established beyond all doubt, by the
history of every one of those numerous revolutions to which the Roman empire and its subsequent divisions have been subjected.

I will therefore only add, in illustration of this
point, that the character of Butler, as depicted by
Schiller, in his Piccolomini and Wallenstein's
Tod, shows well the depth of feeling such minds
are capable of, and the strength of their attachment to their hard-earned honours, as well as
to the power from which they hope to attain
greater; for here, as we know from many examples in history, fiction does not exceed the
reality.

Butler was faithful to the Emperor Ferdinand,
in whose armies he had gained his honours,
until he was made to believe, not only that his
onward course was barred, but that he had been
scorned.   Of this his answer to Count Terzky
is sufficient proof:—

Terzky.

Ihr treffet einen guten Tausch.   Kein Karger,
Kein Ferdinand ist's, dem Ihr Euch verpflichtet,

Buttler (ernſthaft).

Ich biete meine Treu' nicht feil, Graf Terzky,
Und wollt' Euch nicht gerathen haben, mir
Vor einem halben Jahr noch abzudingen,
Wozu ich jetzt freiwillig mich erbiete.
Ja, mich ſammt meinem Regiment bring' ich
Dem Herzog, und nicht ohne Folgen ſoll.
Das Beiſpiel bleiben, denk' ich, das ich gebe.

.   .   .   .

.   .   .   Nun, ſo reut mich nicht
Die Treue, vierzig Jahre lang bewahrt,
Wenn mir der wohlgeſparte gute Name
So volle Rache kauft im ſechszigſten! —
Stoßt euch an meine Rede nicht, ihr Herrn.
Euch mag es gleichviel ſeyn, wie ihr mich habt,
Und werdet, hoff' ich ſelber, nicht erwarten,
Daß euer Spiel mein grades Urtheil krümmt —
Daß Wankelſinn und ſchnell bewegtes Blut,
Noch leichte Urſach' ſonſt den alten Mann
Vom langgewohnten Ehrenpfade treibt.

How he intended to have supported Wallenstein, after he fancied himself unjustly treated by
the emperor, and his determination to revenge
himself on the latter, may be seen from the above,
and is still more apparent from the following :—

Buttler.

.   .   .   .

Mit Allem, was ich hab', bin ich der Eure:
Nicht Männer bloß, auch Geld bedarf der Fürſt.
Ich hab' in ſeinem Dienſt mir was erworben,

Ich leih' es ihm, und überlebt er mich,
Ist's ihm vermacht schon längst, er ist mein Erbe.

His conversation with Octavio, after the latter
had undeceived him, shows the lengths that such
men will go to revenge themselves, and preserve
their name for honour and good faith; while his
answer to Gordon powerfully depicts in a few
words that proud feeling by which they are constantly impelled onwards.

Buttler.

. . . . — Hört und wißt!
Ich bin entehrt, wenn uns der Fürst entkommt.

Gordon.

O solchen Mann zu retten —

Buttler (schnell).
Was?

Gordon.

Ist eines Opfers werth — Seyd edelmüthig!
Das Herz und nicht die Meinung ehrt den Mann.

Buttler (kalt und stolz).

Er ist ein großer Herr, der Fürst — Ich aber
Bin nur ein kleines Haupt, das wollt Ihr sagen.
Was liegt der Welt dran, meint Ihr, ob der niedrig
Geborene sich ehret oder schändet,
Wenn nur der Fürstliche gerettet wird.
— Ein Jeder gibt den Werth sich selbst. Wie hoch ich
Mich selbst anschlagen will, das steht bei mir;
So hoch gestellt ist Keiner auf der Erde,

Daß ich mich felber neben ihm verachte.
Den Menfchen macht fein Wille groß und klein,
Und weil ich meinem treu bin, muß er sterben.*

It is by constantly enlisting in their behalf,
with an uniform policy of which no other nation
furnishes an example, men from *all* classes, with
talented and determined minds, joined to feelings
of this deep nature, that the founders of the
successive dynasties have established themselves
on the throne of China, and this one invariable
feature in the character of its various governments has alone been sufficient to bear the
Chinese empire, in increasing power, through all
the dangers that have in different ages assailed it.

Secondly: *by securing for the government the
services of the wise and talented, public business
must, generally speaking, be efficiently performed.*

It is plain, that in a country where the legislative, judicial, and executive powers, are all exercised by one body, it is of vital importance to
the state that that body be wise and intelligent.
This is so plain with regard to the legislative and
the judicial powers, as to require no illustration;
I shall, therefore, only try to shew, that it is also

* The reader will of course understand that I do not hold
up Butler as a model for imitation. I merely avail myself of
the powerful language of a great poet to illustrate the *depth of
feeling* that the policy of governments must call into play,
either for or against themselves, according as such policy is
good or bad.

of great importance that the executive body, although at first sight a mere agent, should likewise possess talent and capacity. In fact, even in such cases, where every contingency seems to have been anticipated, it is generally found that the executive is required to exercise some judgment, while it frequently happens that the powers of the other two bodies must be largely delegated to it. Now, if an official person be set to the execution of a task, without possessing either natural judgment, or acquired qualifications to fit him for it, he will, in all probability, either fail altogether, or commit a succession of blunders, each requiring to be rectified by an unanticipated exertion of the power of his country. If such country be very powerful, these blunders may pass altogether unnoticed, or, at all events, not be perceived as the real cause of the evils they induce, the more so, as the manner in which the task was executed is generally only known to the public through the account of the person in question. History, however, abounds with instances, some of them very striking, of disastrous events being thus brought about, and from it we may learn how want of good judgment and tact, or even how ignorance of a particular subject, may entail much trouble and extra exertion (not to mention worse consequences), which, if such mismanagement and consequent over exertion be general, will certainly exhaust the strength of a country, as composed of the powers of its individual members. Every such over exertion and exhaustion, whether it takes place in domestic or foreign affairs, serves to undermine the constitution of a state, and renders it unable to compete with an *apparently* weaker but well governed power, the resources of which are husbanded ; just as the strong man who makes a clumsy use of his force, is *in the end* overcome by a weaker but more skilful enemy.

Talent is particularly required in all sorts of negotiations, for then there is generally a trial of wits. A certain penetration to discover the views of the opposite party, an aptitude to acquire a knowledge of his circumstances, in order to ascertain the motives by which he is actuated, and a quick perception of character, to be enabled to humour him, are, as well as that firmness which does not allow of a man's being easily turned aside from his object, all necessary, and are never to be found but with talent. If a man be not possessed of these, he is liable to be sadly outwitted by a clever opponent, to be induced wittingly to give up the objects desired, or to be brought to fancy he has obtained all he wanted, while he has in reality got nothing. This accounts for a disadvantageous treaty having so frequently been the result of a successful war ;

and this is one way by which the resources of a country may be unproductively exhausted, and its ruin gradually brought about, by the incapacity of those to whom its interests are intrusted.

No one acquainted with the negotiations and intercourse of the mandarins with foreigners since the war with England, can for a moment doubt that the natural talent and tact of the former has done their country great service; and we may safely conclude that China is constantly deriving benefit from the principle on which her government is based, in the dealings of her agents with the Tartar hordes to the north and west of her own proper territories.

Thirdly: *the certainty of attaining wealth and rank in the state, merely through personal qualifications, stimulates the* WHOLE *nation to healthful exertions, thus diffusing prosperity throughout it, and multiplying its powers to a great extent.*

There has never been an hereditary aristocracy in China, engrossing to itself, as in several European states of the middle ages, the powers and honours of government—a kind of monopoly that has invariably had a deadening effect on the spirit of nations, being as hurtful in governmental, as mercantile monopolies are in commercial affairs. It is true that there exists a kind of hereditary nobility, attainable by merit, but it is

not from this that government posts* are filled,
and it, moreover, sinks in rank with every new
inheritor, generally becoming extinct in three or
four generations. It is, therefore, evidently
merely an extended application of the principle
in question. That the rank which we attain
should descend in some degree to our grand-
children and their children, will, instead of damp-
ing, only give an additional impulse to the
national spirit of emulation, just as the right
which the law of England allows us of exercising
by will a control over our property, until the
first unborn heir be twenty-one years of age,
instead of weakening, strengthens the tendency
to accumulation. Now in China the poorest
scholar, if he have talent, sees no bounds to his
rise but the throne itself, and instances are constantly occurring of persons raising themselves
from a state of poverty, sometimes from actual
beggary, to very high and lucrative posts. The
emulation that this excites in the acquirement of
that kind of learning requisite to pass the examinations, tends more to the diffusion of knowledge
—a knowledge, too, of many sound principles—
than immense sums spent in charity schools, or
any other system of education, will ever effect;
for the people will not be educated, much less
educate themselves, until the advantages to be

* A few of the military posts excepted.

derived from so doing be made palpable to them.
The all-important cause of national education is,
therefore, intimately connected with the carrying
out of this principle, to which I ascribe so many
other beneficial effects.*

If the Chinese government would open to the
people an equally impartial, and for talent and
bravery an equally certain, path to advancement
through military merit, notwithstanding all that
has been said of Chinese cowardice, I do not
hesitate to assert, that in the course of a very
few years no government in the world would be
able to put itself into a position to dictate to that
of China. The desire of raising himself above
his fellow creatures is one of the strongest passions of man's nature; hence, if even a probability of advancement is held out to him as soon
as he shall be worthy of it, his exertions are
immediately increased; while, if the *certainty*
be there, it is no exaggeration to say that they
are doubled and trebled. Thus it was, that
under the influence of this vivifying incitement,
the half-naked forces of the French republic
were enabled to cope successfully with the well-
provided, twice and three times more numerous,

* Leave, therefore, the money you take from the people, in
order to educate them, in their own pockets, and hold out to
them, on the other hand, sufficient inducements to educate
themselves, and they will do it to a far greater extent, and
infinitely more economically, than you can educate them.

but deadened armies of countries, which the influence of monopoly had reduced to the baneful stationary state; and it was the effect on his soldiers of the judicious use made by Napoleon of this stimulus, as much perhaps as through the talents of the persons raised, that his armies were made capable of such great things.

It would be easy to multiply illustrations, but it seems to me that the above are quite sufficient in support of propositions, the truth of which few or none will be disposed to call in question, and I shall therefore close with the following extract from Vattel, bearing on the subject.

" Il est une autre espèce de justice, que l'on nomme *attributive,* ou *distributive.* Elle consiste en général à traiter un chacun suivant ses mérites. Cette vertu doit régler dans un état la distribution des emplois publics, des honneurs, et des récompenses. Une nation se doit premièrement à elle-même d'encourager les bons citoyens, d'exciter tout le monde à la vertu, par les honneurs et les récompenses, et de ne confier les emplois qu'à des sujets capables de les bien desservir. Elle doit aussi aux particuliers la juste attention de récompenser et d'honorer le mérite. Bien qu'un souverain soit le maître de distribuer ses grâces et les emplois à qui il lui plaît, et que personne n'ait un droit parfait à aucune charge ou dignité; cependant un homme, qui, par une

grande application, s'est mis en état de servir
utilement la patrie, celui qui a rendu quelque
service signalé à l'état, de pareils citoyens, dis-je,
peuvent se plaindre avec justice, si le prince les
laisse dans l'oubli pour avancer des gens inutiles
et sans mérite. C'est user envers eux d'une in-
gratitude condamnable et bien propre à éteindre
l'émulation. Il n'est guère de faute plus perni-
cieuse à la longue, dans un état ; elle y introduit
un rélâchement général ; et les affaires conduites
par des mains malhabiles, ne peuvent manquer
d'avoir un mauvais succès. Un état puissant se
soutient quelque temps par son propre poids, mais
enfin il tombe dans la décadence ; et c'est peut-
être ici l'une des principales causes de ces révolu-
tions, que l'on remarque dans les grands empires.
Le souverain est attentif au choix de ceux qu'il
emploie, tant qu'il se sent obligé de veiller à sa
conversation et d'être sur ses gardes ; dès qu'il se
croit élevé à un point de grandeur et de puissance
qui ne lui laisse plus rien à craindre, il se livre à
son caprice, et la faveur distribue toutes les
places."

It is, then, to the exclusive advancement of
merit and talent, quite independent of every
other principle or doctrine, that the Chinese empire is indebted for its long duration. The doctrine of filial piety, which, in China, enforces an
extreme devotion, not only to parents, but also to

the sovereign as father of the nation, has, it is true, been always one of the engines made use of to secure the obedience of the people, by the influential class of men whose interest it has been the policy of government to identify with its own, and which has, too, reacted on themselves. It will however be, I think, at once allowed me, that the finest doctrines can obtain no influence on the minds of the poor and ignorant, or the unthinking educated classes ; and that even those most consonant to human feelings will gradually lose the hold they may have gained, unless they be constantly inculcated by the example and instruction of some respected body. The Chinese themselves have from the earliest periods been aware of this ; for, in all their writings on government, we find the sentiment continually recurring, that the best laws are of no use if not enforced by the wise and talented, and that such laws cease to operate as soon as men of this class cease to conduct the administration. The policy of all the Chinese dynasties, therefore, whenever we find them in a flourishing state, has been to elevate the only body which could maintain such laws and doctrines, high above every other class of their countrymen ; and whenever any reigning family has deviated from this course, its power has decayed, until it has been finally driven from the throne by the unanimous wish of the nation.

In such cases a temporary dissolution has sometimes taken place; but then, again, the founder
of a new dynasty has at once established himself
on the throne, and upheld the unity of the empire, by recurring to the old characteristic rule of
government; and by thus taking away all temptation to resistance, or separation, from the only
persons who could have successfully opposed him,
or been able to effect any lasting dismemberment.
The very same cause which has obviated any permanent division of the Chinese empire has, with
the increase of population in passing ages, ope-
rated to extend its bounds: it is evident that the
principle referred to, being founded on a never-
failing and, perhaps, the most powerfully-acting
passion of human nature, may be equally applied
in other states, and thus, then, FOR THE RULERS OF
ALL OTHER NATIONS, THE CHINESE EMPIRE CON-
STITUTES A GREAT PRACTICAL LESSON OF FOUR
THOUSAND YEARS' STANDING.

NOTE XII.

ONE of the principal defects of the polity of
the Chinese empire is the existence and operation
of numerous provisions in the code entitled " Code
of the Board of Civil Office for the punishment of the mandarins," whereby the mandarins
are made responsible for a vast number of things
over which they cannot possibly exercise any
control, and in which punishments, more or less
severe, are laid down for them in the case of
failure. The penalties contained in these provisions the mandarins seek, of course, to evade ;
and in doing so, resort to means productive of
great social and moral evils, a few of which I
shall endeavour to point out.

Blackstone, in speaking of arrest by hue and
cry, says : " And, that such hue and cry may
more effectually be made, the hundred is bound
by the same statute, cap. 3, to answer for all
robberies therein committed, unless they take the
felon, which is the foundation of an action against
the hundred, in case of any loss by robbery. By

statute 27 Eliz. c. 13, no hue and cry is sufficient, unless made with both horsemen and footmen. And by statute 8 Geo. 2. c. 16, the constable, or like officer, refusing or neglecting to make hue and cry, forfeits 5l., and the whole ville or district is still in strictness liable to be amerced, according to the law of Alfred, if any felony be committed therein, and the felon escapes. An institution which hath long prevailed in many of the eastern countries, and hath in part been introduced even into the Mogul empire, about the beginning of the last century, which is said to have effectually delivered that vast territory from the plague of robbers, by making in some places the villages, in others the officers of justice, responsible for all the robberies committed within the respective districts." *

I have quoted the passage at length, because its tendency is to propagate what actual facts in China prove to be a very false notion, and which being supported by so high an authority in theoretical law as Blackstone still, it seems, continues to be, is worthy of refutation. By this passage we are taught to believe that offences against the law are prevented, by making the villages and officers of justice responsible for such as are committed within their respective districts.

* Blackstone's Com., book iv. chap. 21.

Now, in reality, the laying the responsibility on the officers of justice is in the highest degree bad ; it tends, in fact, directly to the encouragement of that crime which it is intended to render less frequent; for whether the officers be made responsible for the prevention of crime, or for the apprehension of offenders after its commission, the responsibility implies, in both cases, punishment for want of success; the officers will therefore be constantly on the watch to quash, in the commencement, any proceedings against criminals, in order to prevent the matter coming to light, and thus, though *less will be heard of crime, more of it will exist*, in consequence of the impunity afforded to the guilty.   The daily occurrences in China, where, by a number of provisions in the code above alluded to, the mandarins are rendered responsible in every way, prove this to be beyond all question correct.   The following is one instance :

Some time ago a Chinese merchant, when conveying a cargo of native cotton manufactures in a small vessel along one of the passages of the river which separates the Nan ghai district from that of Shûn tŏ, was attacked by robbers, and had every thing taken from him.   He immediately proceeded to the nearest township magistrate, and presented a petition, accompanied by a fee of two dollars, praying the magistrate to have the

robbers apprehended. Two dollars in the hands
of a mandarin in office is equal to at least 2*l*.
in England, and as the magistrate had just been
appointed, he was somewhat gratified with his
first profits, and, in his ignorance of business and
of his own liabilities, readily promised to take
cognizance of the matter. His mûn-shang, however, who, as my informant (a native of that
township) told me, (his manner changing from one
of ridicule at the mandarin to one of grave
respect,) had formerly served in the yamun of district magistrates, and was a man of experience
and tact: this mûn-shang, who had been out of
the way when the petition was presented, on
hearing of it instantly went to the mandarin,
and represented to him, that this being a case of
open highway robbery, the mandarin in whose
territory it took place was liable to punishment
if he did not succeed in capturing the robbers
within a certain time; and that the best plan
would, therefore, be for him to return the petition,
and refer the complainant to the authorities of
Shûn tŏ; for the water being at that time very
high, extending over a good deal of the surrounding country, it would be difficult to prove that
the robbery had taken place in his township.
This was accordingly done; and as the merchant, in
order to complain to the Shûn tŏ mandarins, must
have travelled about a day's journey over a flooded

country, full of river passages, with a fair prospect
of being referred to some third place on his
arrival, he preferred turning homewards, and so
the matter ended.

Now, in this case, the robbers being rendered
bold by impunity, would be the more ready to
rob again; an industrious man was ruined, and
wherever the story was told, it would have a
discouraging effect on the internal commerce and
manufactures of the country, by making honestly-
gained property insecure, and propagating the
demoralizing and anti-social idea, that it is more
profitable to rob than to work.   And all this had
its rise in that law which makes mandarins responsible for the apprehension of persons com-
mitting a robbery in their district.

In the next following Note, " On Personating
Criminals," the reader will find an instance given
in which the law which makes the mandarins
responsible for the apprehension and punishment
of murderers, led to the deliberate perpetration
of great enormities, and served at once to induce
and justify a general cold-blooded connivance at
them,—a connivance which must demoralize the
nation, and prepare the way for the commission
of other crimes.

In addition to the above examples, I may
mention, that in consequence of certain of those
provisions here objected to, the deliberate starving

to death of prisoners has become a common occurrence. For instance, if the mandarins have apprehended an accessory to a felony, but are unable to get hold of the principal, or where they find that the examination and punishment of certain criminals according to law, would cause the existence of some illegal association to become *officially* known, in which, and in many similar cases, the authorities are liable to punishment, though under the circumstance really blameless—they then order the criminals to be starved to death. In this manner they satisfy the vengeance of the public, while the latter, knowing the onerous liabilities of the mandarins, acquiesce in the proceeding. But the people are thus brutalized, learning to look with apathy, nay, even with delight, upon the cruellest sufferings. After the large fire in the western suburb of Canton, in October, 1843, in which upwards of a thousand Chinese houses and shops, and two of the foreign factories were consumed, several individuals suffered the legal punishment of exposure in the cangue, near the foreign factories; but they were at the same time starved *slowly* to death. An example was considered necessary, in order to prevent the spread of incendiarism; but as the authorities were deterred, by the fear of the penalties, from reporting the actual extent and nature of the disaster, so as to have been

justified in inflicting a severe legal punishment,
they had recourse to this measure. The allowance of food given to the wretches was gradually
reduced, till they all died off (in, as far as I
recollect, about three weeks' time), after passing
through the usual stages of death by starvation.
So long as any were left, there was a small crowd
of people around them, who were not a little
amused by the ravings of such as had become
delirious. Now, I believe, no body of English
people would permit, much less take pleasure in,
the infliction of such a punishment, even though
they had been great losers by the acts of the
criminals.

The brutalization of the hearts of the people
is, however, not the only evil resulting from these
proceedings ; it is easy to understand that the
mandarins will take advantage of the practice,
and the general apathy it induces for the sufferings of others, to employ it for the further-
ance of their own purely selfish schemes against
innocent individuals ; and such is indeed the
case.

The following extract from the above-named
code itself, shows that the Imperial government
is fully aware of some of the evils that result
from making officers liable to punishment, where
there is no guilt, and not even any proven negli-
gence on their part. We should on reading it be

M

much surprised that the objectionable provisions are not all abolished, were it not that we see so many laws and regulations, generally admitted to be prejudicial, in full force in other countries.

The punishments in grave cases of violation of filial duty to be decided on as such cases occur.

On the 7th day of the 8th month of the 18th Kea king * year, the following Imperial edict was received:

" With regard to the memorial sent in by Tûng hsîng, praying that the punishments of the prefects, district magistrates, and higher authorities, within whose jurisdiction grave cases of violation of filial duty occur, might be fixed with rigour, We find that no punishments have hitherto been provided for the officers within whose jurisdictions criminals have committed a violation of filial duty, because, in fact, such criminals—their natures being perfect in cruelty and wickedness— are essentially destitute of all right principles of

* Kea king, Kang he, &c. (in the court pronunciation, Chia chîng, Kang hsi), are not the names of the Emperors usually so called, but of the *period of time* during which they reigned. In like manner, Taou kwang is the name for the present period; and the Chinese, when they say, Taou kwang hwang shang, do not mean " the Emperor Taou kwang," but "the Taou kwang Emperor," i. e. the Emperor of the period of time called " Taou kwang."

human nature ; and punishments can, therefore, only be decided on as the cases occur,* in order to display the power of the national institutions.

" Were more regulations to be established, rigorously fixing punishments for the officials, those on whom the jurisdiction is in such cases incumbent, would, in their dread of these punishments, as awarded by the Board of Civil Office, either not prosecute and punish at all, but each imitate the other in concealing the cases ; or, they would falsify and gloss over the circumstances, avoiding what was grave, and betaking themselves to what was trivial ; and, in thus seeking only to escape punishment, they would, on the other hand, cause the unfilial to escape the penalties of the law by mere chance,—a state of things that would weaken the power of the magisterial institutions, and dissatisfy the human mind.

" Many cases of robbery in the different provinces are concealed, because the local authorities are in constant apprehension of punishment for themselves ; while at present these cases of violation of filial duty are, more than others, reported to us from the different provinces, because the officers, in whose jurisdiction they occur, have

* The meaning of this passage is, that it would be unfair to make the mandarins responsible for the conduct of wretches who are not held back from the commission of atrocities by any of the human feelings that generally serve as a check.

nothing to be careful of or to apprehend in the matter; hence they take measures for the punishment of the malefactors in a spirit of sincerity.

" If the old regulations were to be altered, and additional rules established, it would be nominally governing with strictness in all particulars, but virtually it would be giving rise to abuses proceeding from the measure itself. The said governor, in his memorial, takes a partial view of this subject, and perverts to an extreme degree the idea which should rule in the establishing of laws; it is, therefore, our pleasure that this request be not taken into consideration.

" Then, as to what he says of ' the relations, kindred, neighbours, and constables, being permitted to give information in cases of offences against parents that may happen to occur,' it is also to be feared that such permission would cause much jealousy and ill-will, and a multiplicity of false charges among the lower orders in the villages, so as to give rise to trouble and annoyance. Most decidedly no source of such evils may be created ; and it is, therefore, our pleasure that this particular, also, be not taken into consideration.

" As to the request contained in the memorial, that ' heinous criminals, guilty of a violation of filial duty, be taken to the place where the crime was committed, and undergo the execution of judgment, in order to strike the eye and arouse the mind of the public,' this is feasible, and it is our pleasure that measures be taken in accordance with the request. Respect this."

The Code of the Board of Civil Office for the punishment of the mandarins is faulty in another respect, where it provides gradations in the punishment of a class of offences, to which a sound policy would attach only one. I refer to cases of embezzlement of public money, wilful connivance at criminality, and others of a like nature, all of which ought to be punished with absolute and final dismissal from the government service, in addition to any other penalties such offences might seem to require.

As to the position, that it is injurious to make the villages or districts responsible for offences committed in them ; although the mandarins in special cases will sometimes take bonds from the more respectable people in a town or district, whereby these latter make themselves, to a certain degree, responsible for the non-commission of particular offences; yet, as they will decline doing this where their means of prevention are insufficient, and as the law does not make them responsible, either for the prevention of offences or the apprehension of criminals, I am unable to bring forward any actual occurrences in proof of its correctness.

But at the present day it may be put forth almost as an axiom, that *the object of law is to conceal its own necessary existence from the good citizen, and to make the evil disposed constantly feel that its vengeance is inevitable the moment he becomes criminal.* Now it is certain this twofold object can never be fully attained, but since it is unavoidable that the good citizen should feel the existence of law, he ought, at least, to be made to do so in the least objectionable manner; and it has been fully established by political economists, that the least oppressive manner is that which is regulated on the division of labour.* Let each citizen, then, remain undisturbed in his particular occupation, and let the government main-

* McCulloch, in treating of the division of labour, says: —" It is necessary to bear in mind, that the advantages derived from the division of labour, though they may be, and in fact are, partially enjoyed in every country and state of society, can only be carried to their full extent where there is a great power of exchanging, or an extensive market." This remark, being general, ought to be as applicable to the subject now under consideration as to the production of commodities; and, hence, though the making villages responsible now in England would certainly be bad, it is possible that it may have been necessary in the days of Alfred, when the country was thinly populated, and there was consequently less power of exchanging money for protection.

tain a sufficiently large and efficient police force at the expense of all. This is by far the least burdensome way for them to feel the necessary evil— law ; just as it is cheaper for an individual to provide against the necessity of keeping his feet warm by buying stockings ready made, than it would be for him to spin the yarn and knit the stockings himself. So true is this, indeed, that if any portion of the citizens were to be made specially responsible for that part of the country which they inhabit, they would certainly be gradually led to the maintenance of a police force themselves ; but the history of the police force in England shows that it is much better to have at once some general plan for the whole country.

Another most glaring defect in the existing Chinese institutions, is the totally inadequate pay given to the lower officers, and the low rate at which the salaries of the higher mandarins are fixed ; low, when the wealth and extent of the territories over which they rule are taken into consideration. The table affixed to Note VIII. gives the amount of the salaries allowed to provincial civilians ; and many of them must strike the most cursory observer, as being absurdly small. The mandarins are, in consequence, obliged to gain their incomes by means of extortion, bribery, and illegal fees levied by the yemun, shu-pan and chai-yu. These retain a certain portion themselves, but the greater part goes in different ways to the purses of the mandarins.

Perhaps the total amount of revenue, public and secret, derived by the actual governing power in China, is not larger in proportion than that obtained in England; the great evil is, that by far the most part of it is levied in a very unequal manner, that at once demoralizes the nation, and damps its energies.

The people, knowing that the mandarins cannot possibly live on their salaries, excuse and acquiesce in what I term "illegal fees," i. e. certain tolerably well ascertained sums, which every one who applies to a yamun must pay; and then as a natural consequence, the mandarins take advantage of a system thus endured as a necessary evil, to enforce arbitrary extortions, and oblige people to offer bribes. Hence in the whole country corruption and injustice abound. I believe, in fact, that *all* mandarins take money exclusive of their salary and anti-extortion allowance, and that the grand difference between what the Chinese call the "good" and the "bad" mandarin is, that while the former makes people *pay for justice*,* the latter *sells injustice* to the highest bidder.

Page after page might be filled in pointing out the injuries that result from the low salaries, and the want of any retired allowance; but the most

* As we do in England.

of them are sufficiently obvious, and I shall, therefore, content myself by particularizing one : viz. it renders the mandarins dependent on their clerks and police runners, and obliges them to wink at infringements of the laws, by which they themselves gain nothing. At page 111, the circumstance is mentioned of shu-pan serving after the legal period of five years, and maintaining permanent possession of their posts, merely by changing their names, notwithstanding the mandarin is liable to a heavy punishment for permitting it. The fact is, that if he attempted to put the law in force, which obliges each shu-pan to retire after five years' employment, these men would "strike" in a body ; and, as it requires great experience where so much is false, to levy the illegal income without laying oneself open to conviction or getting into trouble, any new shu-pan who might be employed, would find it very difficult to transact public business, and next to impossible to raise the illegal revenue ; which latter is, of course, under the circumstances, the main object of the mandarin. What has just been stated is not mere surmise. A case actually occurred some time back in Canton, in which a new superintendent of finances, who had at a previous period held a lower post in the province, and then been insulted by a shu-pan, in the superintendent's yamun, and in revenge immediately

forced them to leave on being made superintendent himself, was eventually obliged to receive
them all back again, after putting himself to
much trouble, and making what, in the relative
positions of the parties, amounted to an apology.

A third essential error in the Chinese system
of government is the accumulation of duties
very distinct in their nature, and which we are
in England at great pains to keep separate.
Thus one and the same mandarin is judge, in
matters of life and death, over people from whom
he collects the revenue, and among whom he
also acts as justice of the peace, sheriff, and
coroner,—a system that not only renders extortion and the commission of all kinds of injustice easy and safe, but also entirely precludes
all the well known benefits to be derived from
the division of labour.

The three defects noticed above, are undoubtedly
the most serious in the Chinese polity. Were
they remedied, were the mandarins only punished
when really criminal, and then more rigorously
than at present ; were their salaries sufficiently
raised, and a comfortable competence assured
them in their old age ; and were they educated
for and employed in the discharge of only *one*
class of duties, I firmly believe that the system·
of government in China, considered as a means
of securing the happiness of the people, would,

from certain peculiar beauties it possesses, prove itself, without either juries or parliament, not altogether unworthy of a comparison with those existing in England and France, and much superior to those acted on in Austria, and some other Christian states.

NOTE XIII.

ON PERSONATING CRIMINALS.

THIS is done for money to a great extent in the province of Kwang-tûng, and that frequently in cases involving capital punishment. At first sight the practice appears very extraordinary; for, we ask, what remuneration can compensate a man for the loss of his own life? But, on a little reflection, we perceive that such a practice may not only very easily exist in China, but would probably exist in England also, were those on whom the condemnation of offenders depends subject to punishment if they failed in bringing criminals to justice. Fortunately for the interests of society, our laws are so framed that it would be difficult for any man to sell his life in this way; otherwise, how many unfortunates are there who, with a certain death by starvation staring, not only them, but those still dearer to them than life itself, in the face, would gladly, to obtain a relief for these latter, meet their death a little sooner!

In the department of Ch'au chôu, in the east of Kwang-tûng, a substitute may be procured to confess himself guilty of a felony, and suffer certain capital punishment, for about fifty taels of silver, a sum that would exchange here for about seventeen pounds sterling; and which, valued with reference to the amount of the necessaries of life it would purchase in the department mentioned, is probably not worth more than one hundred pounds sterling in England. Hence it is, that the murder of mandarins and riots are so frequent there; for when a number of individuals of the richer classes are dissatisfied with the conduct of a mandarin, they are never prevented from instigating the lower classes to make disturbances by the fear of personal punishment. In the autumn of 1843, a district magistrate of the Ch'au chôu department being killed in a disturbance, the provincial judge was, in consequence, despatched from Canton, with a force numerically strong, to seize and punish the criminals. He found, however, on his arrival at the scene of the disturbance, a large body of men assembled in arms to oppose him; and the matter was, as frequently happens in such cases in China, ended by a secret compromise.

The gentry, who had instigated the murder of the district magistrate, awed by the force brought against them, bought about twenty substitutes, and bribed the son of the murdered man with, it is said, one hundred thousand dollars, to allow these men to call themselves the instigators, principals, accomplices, &c. The judge, on the other hand, obliged by the Code of the Board of Civil Office to execute somebody, or see himself involved in punishment, and knowing that if he attempted to bring the real offenders to justice, they would employ all their means of resistance, which might easily end in the defeat of his force, and his own death, gave way to these considerations, supported by a bribe, and put the twenty innocent substitutes to death. This is one of many instances in which the pernicious effects of the above-named code for the punishment of the mandarins make themselves apparent. A system of falsehood and corruption has been engendered by it, that is perfectly appalling, and, as in this case, leads frequently to results that cannot be contemplated without a feeling of horror.

NOTE XIV.

ON THE EXTORTIONS AND OPPRESSIONS OF THE MANDARINS.

IN the Note on " The Principal Defects of the Chinese Government," I have pointed out how the wholly insufficient salaries of the mandarins oblige them to draw a private income from the people in a variety of ways, in order to live. And this, if done according to long established customs, not leaving too much to the arbitrary will of those who levy it, is excusable in the eyes of the people. It would, however, be contrary to all experience of human nature to suppose, that when the mandarins have the means of extortion thus placed at their command, they would not be constantly tempted to use them in an oppressive manner ; and they do, in fact, use them to a great extent, and often with such a deliberate cruelty, that the bare recital makes the blood of an Englishman boil. Cases of this sort are, indeed, so frequent, that unless attended with very unusual circumstances, they are not spoken of except by those concerned ; and thus it is, that numerous atrocities pass daily unnoticed here, one single instance of which, in England, would set the whole country in a ferment.

The following, which will give the reader some idea of them, are not related as being among the most flagrant acts of oppression, but merely because they are the only cases of which I happen to have noted the details.

About a year ago, a military mandarin of low rank, stationed near Whampoa, in the course of his extortions, demanded money from the head boatman of a watch-boat, employed by the inhabitants of Whampoa, for the prevention of night-robbery on the river near their town. The boatman, relying on the support of his employers, among whom were several literati, refused to give any thing. The mandarin thereupon induced a man, taken for some trifling offence, to make such declarations in his depositions, as went directly to prove that the boatman had been guilty of robbery, and then issued a warrant for his apprehension. The inhabitants of Whampoa, represented by a literary graduate named Fûng, would not, however, permit the man's being seized, but, knowing him to be innocent, said he should himself go to Canton and demand a trial. This he accordingly did, the graduate Fûng at the same time petitioning the governor-general in his behalf. But the mandarin had already reported the case to his chief, the admiral at the

Bogue, and the latter had written to Canton about it. In addition to this, the mandarins are at all times loath, from a kind of esprit de corps, and a feeling of the necessity of mutual support in their extortions, to aid the people when in opposition to a member of their own class, and were, moreover, at that time, as now, doing all they could to regain the power over the people which they lost through the weakness displayed during the late English war. The consequence was, that, for these various reasons, the death of the unfortunate man was determined on. He was accordingly beaten and otherwise tortured till he confessed himself guilty of the charge brought against him, and soon after executed, with several other equally innocent people who had been implicated in the same manner by the Whampoa mandarin. The graduate Fûng had his degree taken from him—a severe punishment —for having interested himself in behalf of a robber.

In the fourteenth Chia chîng year, A.D. 1809, when the pirates, headed by Chang pau tsai, infested the whole south coast of China, Lin wu, a very rich merchant and shipowner of the Chau chôu district in the eastern part of Kwang-tûng, petitioned the authorities for permission to arm his vessels for self-defence. His petition was granted, but as the number of guns, &c. allowed him was too small, he, without reporting the circumstance, put several more than the authorized number in each of his ships. Eventually, however, he found pirates had such a complete command of the coast, and were so numerous, that it was folly to think either of evading or resisting them, and therefore ordered his vessels to pay the black-mail demanded, amounting, it is said, to several thousand of taels. On payment of this they got a passport, which enabled them to make that one voyage without further molestation. As people of smaller capital did not like to risk it at all on the sea under such circumstances, a great deal of trade fell into the hands of this Lin wu, whose profits derived from this species of monopoly were, again, so great as to permit his paying for each of his vessels large fees with a regularity that secured him an immunity from farther annoyance or exactions. Matters continued in this state till 1812, when the pirate chief, Chang pau tsai, was bribed by the offer of a military mandarinship * to give up piracy; after which he

* This proceeding, to us so extraordinary, is usual in such cases in China, and is merely an extended application of the principle on the operation of which the stability of the empire rests. The system of government examinations opens a road by which *most* men of talent can advance to distinguished positions, at once satisfying their ambition and supporting government; but when any one, unable from circumstances to rise thus, forces himself up into power in another way,

exerted himself so much to apprehend his old associates, that the sea became comparatively safe; and Lin wu, no longer enjoying his old monopoly with its high profits, sold his vessels and retired from business. Unfortunately for himself, however, he stored his extra guns and other arms in his own house, where they were often seen by the intendant of the Ghwui chôu chia circuit, the one in which the Chau chôu district is situated. This mandarin, who is remembered as Wu a to, Wu the hump-backed, had, on assuming office, made diligent inquiries as to who were the richest people of his circuit, and had from that time honoured Lin wu with a very intimate friendship. In 1813, an Imperial edict was received promoting him to the post of provincial judge for Kwangtûng; and, on taking leave of his friend Lin wu, he asked the latter for a loan of 100,000 taels to defray the expenses (bribes, gratuities, &c.) he would incur on arriving at Pekin, in order to have the customary audience before entering on the duties of his post. Although Lin wu must have been well aware that it was highly dangerous to make an enemy of such a powerful mandarin as the provincial judge, still the sum demanded was

and by opposing the government, this latter, as soon as it plainly perceives, from its own inability to subdue him, that he is really a man whose talents render him a dangerous enemy, immediately enlists him on its own side.

so large, that he, knowing he would probably get only a small portion, if any, of it back again, answered that he had only about 15,000 taels in hand, and would require some time to get together so large a sum as that required. Wu, the judge, on receiving this answer, went off in a great rage, and, as soon as he had entered on the duties of his post at Canton, accused Lin wu to the governor-general as a person who had been in combination with the pirates, stating that the great and small arms used were still in his house Orders were immediately issued to the local mandarins to apprehend and send him to Canton. On his arrival here he was first examined at the yamun of the district magistrate of Nan ghai; afterwards at that of the prefect of Kwang-chôu, where he was several times examined with torture; and, lastly, at that of his old friend Wu, the provincial judge, who deputed a lower mandarin to examine him. In this last place he was subjected to all the customary tortures, till " there was not a whole place left in his skin." He, however, had fortitude enough to hold out, and constantly refused to confess himself guilty of the crime laid to his charge; he could not, therefore, be put legally to death, and was remanded to prison. He probably could, and would have obtained his liberty at the expense of his wealth, but he thought it better to employ a part of this latter in giving effect to an accusation against Wu a to, then being presented by his brother at the Imperial court. His Imperial majesty, on the case being brought to his knowledge, instantly dispatched a special commissioner to Canton to examine into it. The judge, on hearing of this, perceiving that if the commissioner found Lin wu alive, the matter might easily end in his own ruin, immediately instructed the two district magistrates of Nan ghai and Pan yŭ, resident at Canton, to examine him again in his (the judge's) own yamun, and at the same time employed the different means at his disposal, to induce the clerks, who had to take the deposition, *to note a confession*. In this he succeeded ; the district magistrates winked at the proceeding ; the governor-general, on the report of the judge, issued the death-warrant; and a few days afterwards Lin wu was taken in the grey of the morning to the place of execution and beheaded. As he passed through the streets, the people heard him in their beds making known his story in a loud voice, and telling them not to exert themselves to make money, for if they did, they would either have to give it to the mandarins, or suffer the same fate he was going to meet. When the commissioner arrived, and found the man dead, while his confession, made before the two district magistrates, was presented to him, he could do nothing but return, and so the matter ended.

About two years ago the following case occurred. A man from one of the northern provinces, who had formerly been a tea-merchant, but, having lost his money, had settled in Canton as a doctor, and resided for several years in a respectable street in the western suburb, was returning home one day at noon, when he was, at the distance of about 100 paces from his own door, attacked by five men, two of whom held his hands, while one seized him by the throat and stopped his mouth, and the remaining two robbed him of a watch and twenty taels of silver he had about him. It was done in an instant, but as he shouted, thieves! the moment his mouth was free, the neighbouring shopmen, who had been attracted by the struggle, but had not had time to see what was actually going on, succeeded in capturing one of the fellows. This man the doctor had, according to the advice of his friends, taken to the nearest temple, and then called the householders of his street, by beat of gong, to a consultation. They admitted that as the doctor was an inhabitant of their street, and had been robbed in it in open day, the matter was a public one, concerning them generally; and intimated to him their readiness to disburse, according to their custom, one half of the expense of handing the prisoner over to the mandarins, if he (the doctor) would pay the other half.   This he agreed to do, and as some of the householders had friends in the yamun of the local military mandarin, which is situated in the same suburb, the prisoner was taken there, and received on payment of about three dollars as fees.   The mandarin, a lieutenant, handed the prisoner over to the district magistrate of Nan ghai, as the local civil authority, at the same time sending in a report to his superior officer, showing that *he* had captured the man. The latter on being examined by the district magistrate, declared that the doctor owed him money, and would not pay him, and as he belonged to a gang that was connected with the yemûn of the district magistrate, the matter ended in the doctor's being summoned to the yamun, detained there ten days, and, far from recovering his stolen money and watch, only liberated after paying about fifteen dollars, while the robber was set free unpunished.

It may be remarked here, for the satisfaction of the reader, that the above stories, as well as the others contained in these Notes, were not related expressly in order to illustrate any particular subject, but are merely a few of the many told me incidentally when talking of other matters.   For instance, when one day explaining to a Chinese how our doctors were educated, I happened to speak of the smell in the dissecting rooms. "Ah!" said he, "the smell of human corpses is very peculiar,—like nothing else; in the neighbourhood of our prisons you sometimes feel it very strong." "How does that happen?" asked I. "Why," replied he, "the gaolers don't report the death of the prisoners, but let their bodies lie there for a day or two sometimes." "But what is their object in this?" asked I, unable to perceive why people should keep putrid corpses lying close to their own dwellings. "The gaolers make a little money by it," said he, "coffins for persons who die in prison are charged in the public accounts, one being of course allowed for each body. Now when the gaoler sees that one of his prisoners is dead, he looks round to see if there be not another about to die. If there be such other, he waits till he is dead too; he then reports them, charges for two coffins, but," continued my friend, the tears, as is usual with the Chinese in relating such cases of misery, streaming from his eyes from excessive merriment, "has both the corpses squeezed into one. The prisoners are generally nothing but bones with skin on them, and two can be put very well into one coffin. The coffins are very coarse, but the gaoler gains after all about a dollar, or a dollar and a half in this way."

Now here I got, quite incidentally, a piece of information concerning a very curious method of turning a penny at the expense of government, and which throws some light on the state of the Chinese prisons.

In addition to the desire of direct gain, the mandarins have another, likewise selfish, motive for the commission of injustice and cruelty.

When robberies, murders, &c., occur, it is incumbent on them, by law, to apprehend—to convict the criminals. If they fail in doing this they are punished, while, if they succeed, they are sometimes rewarded. Hence, if a case of this nature be brought to the notice of the mandarin in such a manner as does not permit of its being hushed up, he becomes at once very anxious to find criminals and get it settled. But in China (as in Bavaria) a man cannot be convicted, or at least judgment pronounced against him and executed, until he has confessed himself guilty; on the other hand, the mandarins can torture the accused for prevarication and to extort a confession, where he is plainly guilty. Now, although the mandarin is liable to punishment if it should be proved that he has employed torture unnecessarily or unjustly, yet, all circumstances considered, it is easy to perceive that the innocent *accused* has in every case much to dread, and that if there be any circumstantial evidence, tending to shew him guilty, he has a very poor chance of escape. The mandarin, whose chief aim is less to do justice than to find a criminal, aided by the advice of his shï ye, repeatedly examines the accused with and without torture, employing every means in his power to entrap or force the latter into an admission, tending directly to prove his guilt. Sometimes the mandarin flatters—tells the prisoner he is an intelligent, clever man; wonders how *he* could have done such and such a thing, &c. &c.; at other times he threatens and bullies, tells the prisoner he is talking stuff, that he is a fool, cuckold, vagabond, &c., and that he will condemn him to death. If these means do not succeed, the accused is kept kneeling (the position in which he is examined) on his bare knees till they are raw, and is beaten on the posteriors, hands, and face ; so that, even if he be quite innocent, his escape depends chiefly on his possessing powers of endurance such as few human beings are gifted with.

NOTE XV.

ON THE INTERNAL STABILITY OF THE CHINESE EMPIRE.

A QUESTION that very naturally occurs to the mind of every one on repeatedly hearing of acts of oppression and injustice, such as are described in the last Note, and one which the reader is probably at this moment ready to ask is, how can the government of a country where such a state of things exists maintain itself? Most people, on reflecting on the long duration of the Chinese as a nation, and on remarking farther the present apparent stability of the government, and the great amount of cheerful industry* among the people, are led to conclude that such acts of injustice and cruelty as I have detailed, do *not*

---

* The reader must not suppose from what he hears of the industry of the Chinese that they continue their exertions so long as the English, much less that they are equally enterprising. The Chinese, especially after having gained a moderate competence, enabling them to live comfortably and give their children a good education, generally stop short in their onward course, the certainty of being allowed to enjoy the fruits of their exertions and risks not being sufficiently great to induce them to proceed beyond a certain point.

take place, but exist only in the imaginations of those who have described them. But the conclusions to which we arrive by reasoning, cannot be maintained against well established facts; when we, therefore, hear numerous instances of deliberate injustice and shocking cruelty, related with all their details as matters of evidently too frequent occurrence to excite indignation in the minds of the narrators,—when similar instances have come under our own notice, the above question recurs in full force to our minds.

Now, when it becomes but too palpable that much oppression exists in any particular country, yet at the same time its government, with a very despicable physical force at its disposal, is able to maintain itself in spite of internal commotions, and the people, further, display a considerable amount of voluntary mental and physical exertion, it is manifest that there must be contained in the institutions of that country, some principle or principles constantly operating to counteract and overbalance the usual effects of long continued injustice and tyranny on the part of the rulers. In the case of China, I must refer the reader to that principle, to the working of which I have ascribed the long duration of the Chinese empire,* viz. that the essence of good government con-

* See Note XI., of which the present may indeed be regarded as an amplification.

sists in the elevation of talent and ability only to office.

Should the reader be disposed to think that I lay too much weight on the operation of this principle, I would beg him to recall to his mind that the actual state of countries depends *mainly* on the feelings and sentiments of their inhabitants, as modified by, and modifying, their institutions, the natural advantages of their territories having but a secondary influence; and that all important revolutions in nations have their rise in the passions of the individuals who form them, and that it therefore follows, that if the feelings and passions of *all* the individuals composing a people be systematically acted upon, in one fixed manner, *some* important results must ensue; while, if it should so happen that a passion, of which not a human being is destitute, and which in a great proportion of mankind bears down every other before it, be in all individuals carefully and constantly called forth into full play in aid of the government, it is plain no *internal* commotion will ever overturn such a government. Now the passion on which the principle referred to, in the case of China, is based—*the desire of distinguishing oneself among one's fellow creatures*— is not only universal, but is in most individuals the strongest of all those inherent in human nature. Parental and filial affection, brotherly

love, the love of the sexes, the love of country,
even the love of life itself, both in past and present times, have been made, not merely to yield
before it, but entirely to evacuate the human breast
to its uncontrolled sway.   Scarcely one action of a
man's life does not proceed from it.   The soldier,
when he encounters an almost certain death in
some extraordinary deed of daring ; the scholar,
when he ruins health in unremitting study ; the
fop, when he spends an hour in tying, untying,
and retying his neckcloth ; and the ruffian, when
he, among his admiring associates, affects a coarse-
ness still greater than that given him by nature ;
are all acting under the influence of this one
passion.

Let us now consider more particularly how the
principle operates in China, to prevent the people
rising against the government, and to render
ineffectual such commotions as are actually called
into existence by oppressions, marked with more
than the usual injustice and cruelty on the part
of the mandarins.

A great number of the only class of individuals
whose abilities would enable them, if subjected
to such oppressions, speedily to overturn the
government, are, by the existing system of public
examinations, continually raised above all oppression, and become, in fact, the parties who commit it : a still greater number hope to raise them-

selves to the same position, and are, together with
their relations, thus induced to endure such evils
patiently, rather than seek to overthrow a government, the characteristic feature of which is a
system they hope eventually to derive more personal advantages from than would be sufficient
to compensate them for what they suffer. With
this latter body, the literati, rising scholars, and
their nearer relations, the actual holders of office,
the mandarins, are, too, always obliged to be
somewhat more scrupulous and tender in their
dealings. Hence the only class which the mandarins have to repress and overcome by force, is
composed of persons who have either no natural
ability, or are too poor to procure an education,—
persons who, with a moderate proportion of talented and educated leaders, would, from their
number and their desperation, be formidable
indeed ; but left as they are to themselves, only
break out into tumults and insurrections, which,
like the Jacquerie in France, the insurrection of
the common people in the minority of Richard
II. in England, and those that prevailed in the
south of Germany and in Hungary during the
end of the fifteenth, and the first quarter of the
sixteenth centuries, are ultimately put down with
terrible loss to themselves, after some well-de-
served punishments have been inflicted, and some
ravages committed by them at the first outbreak.

In the European insurrections just alluded to, the *immediate* cause of suppression was in general the force brought against the insurrectionary bodies; but when we reflect that these latter, besides being comparatively large, were composed of hardy men, animated by the courage of despair, we cannot but believe that the original and main causes of their want of success were of a moral nature.

In China, in addition to the absence of talent and knowledge on the side of the insurrectionists, it so happens that the education, which the promotion of talent and ability only to the honour and wealth conferred by office diffuses so extensively, is of a nature which tends materially to prevent ideas of resistance spreading among the people. Every man is induced to learn himself, and infuse anxiously into the minds of his children, from their earliest infancy, a set of doctrines all inculcating the duty of patient endurance, the necessity of subordination, and the beauty of a quiet orderly life. The feelings with which the people are thus imbued, would not of course, be sufficient of themselves to prevent a successful rise against the cruel oppressions actually existing; but they help to do so, and in every case they give a speedier effect to the power, moral and physical, which is put in motion to suppress commotions; for it is only very strong, and therefore very rare minds that are able to offer a continued practical resistance to the deep impressions of early youth.

It may, however, be observed here, that in a country where neither juries nor a parliament exists, and where the mandarins generally support each other very zealously in opposition to the people, the fear of the latter being driven to rise against them is the main check on their arbitrary proceedings. When the people rise, as they from time to time do, they frequently put the local mandarins to death; if not, then the latter become, in consequence of the tumults, amenable to some of the provisions of the "Code for the punishment of the mandarins," and, as a general rule, an affair of this sort proves highly detrimental to the official career of those most implicated in it. In the instances of revolts in various countries of Europe mentioned above, the histories tell us that the condition of the lower classes was rendered still worse by their efforts to better themselves. But there is much reason for believing that, although nominally, as the law on paper existing would show it, they might be in as bad a state as ever, yet their condition must, in consequence of a change in the manner of exercising privileges conferred by law or custom on their superiors, have been in reality considerably ameliorated. In all these insurrec-

tions of the common people, great numbers of
their oppressors, and of the class they belonged
to, suffered both in life and property ; and it
is difficult to conceive that the terrible lessons
which were administered in this way could have
altogether been forgotten. The following case
will illustrate my meaning.

A few years ago an occurrence took place in
Mecklenburg, which excited some sensation at the
time. It appears that a body of the peasantry,
a class in the two duchies, who, if no longer
actually bondsmen, since their dukes declared
them free in 1820, are still, it would seem, in
consequence of the depressed state from which
they have not yet been able to raise themselves,
very much at the mercy of certain land-stewards ;
—a body of these men, exasperated beyond endurance by the cruel oppressions of the steward
of the estate they lived on, got hold of the fellow,
stripped him naked, and forced him to dance on
broken glass till he died, they themselves sitting
smoking around. Such, at least, was the story current at the time in the north of Germany. Now,
supposing it to be correct, and supposing, what in
such a case doubtless actually happened, that the
perpetrators of the deed suffered a severe punishment, it would yet be difficult to conceive that
the condition of the peasantry generally has not
by this act been materially improved in fact,

whatever it may be nominally, at least as far as these land-stewards are concerned. To dance naked on broken glass into what, we are bound to believe, would, for persons who delight in the miseries of their fellow-creatures, only prove a worse state, is not pleasant ; and the reflection on the *possibility* of being called on to perform in that way, can scarcely fail to have a salutary influence on minds inclined to brutal oppressions.

The very unfair proportion of Manchoos employed by the present dynasty in government posts, is a deviation from the fundamental principle of Chinese polity ; and, as might be expected, it constantly nourishes a feeling of dissatisfaction among the Chinese, which, though they are obliged to be at some pains to conceal it, occasionally escapes them. The selling of government posts, which has recently been carried to a great extent, is another deviation from it, dangerous in the highest degree for the present rulers. Hitherto the dread of the more warlike Manchoos, joined to the partial operation allowed to this principle, has been sufficient to repress or prevent the general rising of a quiet-loving people ; but if the practice of selling offices be continued, in the extent to which it is at present carried, nothing is more likely, now that the prestige of Manchoo power in war has received a severe shock in the late encounters with the English, than that a Chinese Belisarius will arise, and extirpate or drive into Tartary the Manchoo garrisons or bannermen, who, during a residence in China, twice as long as that of the Vandals in Africa, have greatly deteriorated in the military virtues ; while they still retain enough of the insolence of conquerors, to gain themselves the hatred of the Chinese.

NOTE XVI.

ON SOME OF THE MORE PROMINENT FEATURES IN
THE CHARACTER AND MANNERS OF THE CHI-
NESE; AND ON THE BEST METHOD OF DEALING
WITH THEM.

THERE are few things so difficult as to describe
the character of a people in such a manner as to
convey to the mind of a person who never saw
them something like a correct idea of it. When
a man, practically acquainted with their language,
has lived for a long time with them on terms of
intimacy, he himself begins to understand their
genius; and if you put a case to him, and ask how
they would feel and act under the circumstances
given, he would probably be able to tell you with
considerable precision; but if their feelings and
actions, as predicted by him, should be irrecon-
cileable with your experience of other nations,
appearing improbable, if not altogether absurd,
and you were to ask this man for an explication
—for a statement of the grounds from which he
drew his conclusions—he would most likely be
quite unable to give you any thing of the sort,
but would merely make general assertions to the

effect that "so the thing was." He is himself only conscious of *feeling* how the people would feel and act; but the fact is, he has in constantly associating with them observed, and his mind has, without any distinct intention, treasured up, a great variety of incidents, speeches, and peculiarities of manner, trifling and important, which serve to him, without his being fully aware of it, as precedents and data, guiding him in forming his judgments with greater or less certainty, according as they are numerous and fully understood, or otherwise. I am, therefore, fully convinced—the more so as a man in the position described can seldom express *all* he feels—that the best way of imparting to the mind of another person a correct idea of the genius of a foreign people, would be to hand him for perusal a collection of notes, formed by your having carefully recorded great numbers of the incidents that had attracted your attention, particularly those that struck you as at all extraordinary, with the explanation obtained from natives accounting for that which you regarded as extraordinary; and by your having taken down, in like manner, a number of the generally current stories, no matter whether actually true or not; for no stories would be generally current that were not *true in spirit*; that is to say, in accordance with the ideas and feelings of the people.

I regret now, when I come to publish these Notes, that my avocations have not left me time to make such a collection as that just described, for it would, doubtless, have been much more satisfactory to the reader than the following conclusions, notwithstanding that they are drawn from what would have constituted it.

The imperfections of human language increase the difficulties that lie in our way, when we would give a description, at once short and correct, of national character. Thus it is both true and false to say, that the Chinese people possess a high degree of *fortitude*. It is true, in so far as fortitude signifies, *that quality of the mind which enables a man to bear pain or adversity, without murmuring, depression, or despondency.* And false, in so far as it means, *that quality which enables him to meet danger with readiness and courage.* Though the minds of the Chinese will, of course, give way to very great suffering, I have frequently had occasion to admire the manner in which they will meet any unavoidable evil. They regard it full in the face as it were, after which they resign themselves to their fate almost with a degree of cheerfulness, seemingly determined to make the best of circumstances as they are. On the other hand, they have but little courage. But here again, it is necessary to make a distinction. Taken as individuals of the human race, the Chinese possess doubtless, as much of *constitutional* or *animal courage*, as any other specimens of it; but of that courage which is based on a determination of the mind to display intrepidity, they are nationally wanting, simply because their own opinions and institutions offer little inducement to their minds to come to any such determination. In England we are in our childhood taught, on Sundays by examples contained in the Jewish history, on week-days by examples taken from the histories of all countries, and collected in our school books, to regard bravery and warlike talents as among the highest of human qualities, as certain to excite the respect of our fellow countrymen, and likely to raise their possessors to honour and wealth. In China, on the contrary, the national education tends rather to reduce the military virtues to a low place in the estimation of human beings, as the following extracts from the universally studied " Four Books "* sufficiently prove.

" To teach men," said Confucius, " with a patient, mild spirit, and not to revenge unreasonable conduct, constitutes the valour of the south, *and is the constant habit of the man of superior virtue.* To lie under arms, and fearlessly meet death, is the valour of the north, and the element of the valiant man."

* See Collie's Translation.

" Tsze loo asked whether the superior man esteemed valour ? Confucius replied, The superior man considers justice of the first importance."

" Seuen, king of Tse, in answer to Mencius, who was praising the beauty of peace, said: Exalted words! I, poor man, have an infirmity; I love valour. Mencius replied, I entreat your majesty not to love low valour. If a man strike his sword, and, with a fierce countenance, call out, Who will oppose me? this is the low valour of a common man. He then points out, as an example of a truly brave man, a certain Wan wang who had succeeded by his interposition in preventing a war just on the point of commencing."

" Mencius said, Those who wrangle and fight for territory, and fill the wastes with dead bodies, and who fight for cities so as to fill the cities with dead bodies, may be said to lead on the earth to eat human flesh. Death is not a sufficient punishment for such crimes. Hence those who delight in war deserve the highest punishment."

" Mencius said, When a man says, I know well how to draw up an army, I am skilled in fighting, he is a great criminal."

Now let the reader imagine to himself soldiers and officers *deeply imbued* with such doctrines as these, badly clothed, paid, and armed, with little or no prospect of pension in case of disability from old age or wounds, opposed to well-fed and well-clothed English troops, who *know* that their arms are the most efficient in the world, that they have all the advantages of a most perfect discipline, who moreover never doubt that if wounded they will be as sedulously cared for as circumstances will permit; and that, if disabled, they will receive a pension sufficient to enable them to live comfortably in their station in society; let the reader bring this fully before his mind, and he will not be surprised at the former being beaten into flight by the latter after a mere show of resistance.

The Chinese are known to possess a great command over their tempers; and we often see instances of their bearing with the greatest apparent equanimity injuries and insults which would make an European ungovernable. It must not be supposed, however, that this proceeds from cowardice. It arises from their really considering

self-command a necessary part of civilization;
while they regard passionate conduct and a hasty
temper as indecent, and giving evidence of a low
nature. This having for ages been an established
doctrine with them, it has become a characteristic
of the people to suffer insults and injuries patiently.
But it would be well for those who are in the
habit of displaying their valour—a valour completely repressed in England by a salutary fear of
fists—by insulting and abusing the Chinese, to
bear in mind that these latter are often prevented
from resenting their conduct instantly more from
the fear of the scene that would ensue, and the
bad character it would procure them, than from
fear of the consequences of a personal encounter.*

For this quality, and for another now to be
noticed, *the readiness they evince to yield to the
force of reason*, the Chinese certainly deserve to be
considered a highly civilized people. They settle
their disputes more by argument than by violence. That many, when they have a particular
object in view, will continue to cavil after they

* It would be unreasonable to say any thing against a man
for resenting gratuitous insults on the part of the Chinese,
when (as is the case in Canton, where such insults abound)
it is impossible to obtain redress by law. But it is evident
there is a vast amount of bravery displayed in beating the
Chinese without just cause, particularly at Hong-kong, which
would never dare to shew itself in England, and which does
very much to hurt our interests.

themselves plainly see they are in the wrong, there can be no doubt; but there is much less of this conduct to be met with in China than probably in any other country. The Chinese who would persist in it could not fail to get a character so bad as would prove highly detrimental to his own interests. A Chinese placard posted at the street corners, exposing the unreasonable, i. e. unequitable conduct of a party in any transaction is, if the want of equity be sufficiently proved, to the full as effective, if not more so, than a similar exposure of an Englishman in a newspaper. This has its rise, however, partly from the circumstance, that it is not so easy to obtain justice by law here as in England; which naturally leads a society to inflict for its own sake an indirect punishment on offenders by tacit universal agreement.

What is said above refers chiefly to the conduct of the Chinese among themselves. Many foreigners would probably see little of the quality for which I have given them credit; but though it is too plain that their treatment of us is often quite unreasonable, yet the foreigner must not forget, when he judges of their conduct in particular cases, to free his mind from such European notions as are *merely* conventional, but which, from possessing an universal authority among us, may easily be confounded with the

rules of natural justice.   It is by the latter alone,
of which the Chinese have in general a very correct knowledge, that they should be judged ; and
some allowance should be made for their thraldom
to their own peculiar conventional notions.

Judged in this manner, and with reference to
the trait now under consideration, a readiness to
appreciate and yield to clear reasoning based on
equity, the Chinese character presents itself in a
very favourable light, and it was, I doubt not,
chiefly to this that Sir Henry Pottinger referred,
when, in his speech at Liverpool, he bestowed
very high praises on the Chinese, and termed
Chi ying an " enlightened " statesman.

I may remark here, that the state of society in
China countenances the opinions of those who
maintain that duelling is unnecessary.   Bullies
seem to be kept in check here by the force of
public opinion, and the Chinese neither fight duels,
nor, though murders occur as in England, can
they be said to assassinate or poison.

The practical hold that the doctrine of filial
piety, as taught in China, has taken on the minds
of the people, is the cause of a characteristic
feature in the national genius.   As the Chinese
sages and wisest statesmen have always pointed
out the reward of talent and merit as the grand
rule for good government, so they have always
insisted, that the best system of national instruc-

tion is that founded on the doctrine of filial piety.
This doctrine has, from the remotest ages to the
present time, been sedulously taught by the pre-
cept and example of the most able men in the
country, and enforced by the power of the ruler,'
exercised by these same men.   This, together
with the circumstance, that a most intimate
acquaintance with all the sages have said about
this doctrine is necessary to every man who
would rise, accounts for its widely extended
and great influence; and as it requires a quite
unnatural degree of devotion and reverence on
the part of the children, it may fairly be considered as forming the religion of the Chinese.
Every people, from the nature of the human
mind, must have *a* religion, pointing out a highest
duty.   Our religion is comprised in the two commands, "Do to others as you would be done by,"
and "Fear God."   The latter contains our highest
duty, but of it the Chinese may be said to know
nothing.   The chief command of his religion is,
"Love, honour, and obey your parents," and to
say or to do any thing against it, is as shocking
and as disgusting to the feelings of a Chinese, as
blasphemy to those of a Christian.   It is, in fact,
Chinese blasphemy; for, the parents of a Chinese
being holy to him, and it being his most sacred
duty to honour them, to him *God* is *parent*, and
parental is divine.   I believe it is only by view-

ing it in this light that we can fully comprehend the Chinese doctrine of filial piety.

The Chinese are as capable of feeling a deep gratitude for disinterested services rendered them as any people. This, the many instances of gratitude, expressed at the risk, or even with the loss of life, which occur incidentally in their stories, and the way in which such instances are passed over by the narrators, as matters of course, prove beyond all doubt. They are capable of forming strong attachments, too, in domestic relations, as among kindred, or between servant and master ; but it must be confessed, they seem to be in general almost void of philanthropy, while many of them are able to perpetrate the greatest cruelties unmoved. This indifference to the sufferings of their fellow creatures, the existence of which I can only account for, by supposing the cruel punishments inflicted by their rulers to have brutalized their minds, is decidedly the most disagreeable feature in their character. Their feeling of superiority, when it shows itself unintentionally through a polite demeanour, is rather amusing than otherwise; and when it assumes the shape of open arrogance, it can be checked, and a kind of pity felt for their ignorance ; but their apathy for human misery creates, as often as observed, an unmitigable feeling of dislike. They even seem, in some measure, gra-

tified by the distresses of others. They almost
invariably laugh when speaking of the death of
people known to them, and even of those they
called their friends. "So and so is, I have just
been informed, dead; he was a very old friend of
mine: we were at school together. I am going
to his house to-night to cry over him." This is
by no means an unusual speech for a Chinese,
which he delivers with a smiling happy face, as if
talking of his friend's approaching wedding.

When once speaking to a Chinese of the re-
munerations for pilots in England being fixed by
government, he gave me a description of the
wreck of a junk, in consequence of the exorbitant demands of the pilots, who, seeing signs of a
coming typhoon, demanded more than the master
of the vessel could make up his mind to give.
It being at the time nearly dark, the latter,
hoping the typhoon would not come on before the
ensuing day, anchored, with the intention of
sounding his way into the river he wished to
enter, as soon as it was light again. The next
morning, however, he was caught in the storm;
the junk struck on a hidden rock, was driven off
again, and began rapidly to fill. The sailors
nearly all took to the water-butt, which, loosened
from the vessel, is the usual refuge in such cases.
The master proposed saving himself on the large
sail—which, being composed of matting, extended

on and supported by a number of bamboos running across it, is very buoyant—and for this purpose cut away, as he supposed, all the ropes which attached it to the vessel. Unfortunately, however, he had not done so completely, and when the junk went down, he was gradually drawn down with the sail and drowned. The water-butt went down also soon after, so that only two or three men saved themselves by clinging to loose pieces of timber.

Now, most Englishmen, on telling this story, would feel a little commiseration for the sufferers, and few, if any, would be excited to laughter by it; but the Chinese narrator no sooner came to speak of the drowning, than he began to laugh, and he was so particularly tickled by the manner in which the master met his death, that the tears ran from his eyes from excess of merriment, and he could scarcely get on with the tale.

While this story illustrates the want of humane feelings on the part of the Chinese, the cause of its being related is, however, an instance of the candour with which they will admit any thing in foreign countries to be of a superior nature, as soon as they perceive it, even though it should be the existence of a government institution which they have not.

The practice of mutilating children, and constraining them to act as beggars, in order to gain

a livelihood, by taking from them the gifts their
forced pertinacity or disgusting appearance ex-
torts from the public, exists to a great degree in
Canton. All the blind people who are seen in
the neighbourhood of the factories are, I am
told, victims of a system that constitutes a strong
proof of cruelty in a people who suffer its existence among them.

The practice of infanticide exists here, as the
bodies of infants floating occasionally on the river
sufficiently prove; but it may be fairly doubted,
whether there is very much more of it than in
England. It has been stated above that the
Chinese are capable of forming strong attachments in domestic life, and it seems indeed as if
they concentrated their affections on those more
immediately connected with them; hence, often
having remarked instances of *deformed female*
children being treated with constant and evident
affection by their parents, members of the boat
population, I am inclined to believe, that when
infants are put to death, it is solely because their
parents are altogether unable to support them.

Notwithstanding that the Chinese have so few
hereditary titles, that they may be said to have
no nobility, in so far as that word signifies an
order of men holding definite positions above the
lower and middle classes, and deriving their rank
and station from birth, there exists nevertheless

a great deal of ancestral pride among them. In a certain sense all families are, of course, alike old; but if we understand by an "old and noble family," the *lineal* descendants, in a respectable station of life, of some celebrated man, the Chinese have among them older and more noble families than any western nation. The Kung family, i. e. the lineal descendants of Confucius, whose surname was Kung, has been pointed out as an instance of this, and indeed the oldest and highest European families sink into insignificance before it. The great ancestor of the Kung lived 550 years before Christ, about 200 years after the foundation of Rome, and before the Roman state assumed the form of a republic. The reader must remember that no parallel can be drawn between him and Mahomet, or the founder of any religion. Confucius never pretended, either directly or indirectly, to any superhuman powers, or intelligence with superior beings; he was neither a fanatic nor an impostor, but simply a moral philosopher and a statesman, and his doctrines have obtained their present great authority, merely because they are generally sound. There cannot be a doubt that it is to the influence of one of them, this immense empire owes its existence in its present state; and when we reflect on this, we cannot help considering Confucius as one of the most illustrious men that ever lived, and acknowledging that the Kung, many of whom now hold high offices in the state, have just claims to be considered the oldest and most noble family in the world. But, besides this, there are many other noble and very old families in China. It is true that their nobility does not consist in the possession of hereditary titles, large unalienable estates, or peculiar privileges,* and they may be for several generations unheard of, but the members of them are not the less proud of their birth ; and every now and then some talented man among them will, by his own exertions, raise himself to a high post in the state, and thereby revive the ancient glory of his name. The picture of a man of this sort is then carefully preserved by his descendants, and has honours paid to it at certain times, with those of their other celebrated ancestors.

I would not be understood to say that there is more or even as much of family pride among the Chinese as among the hereditary nobles of England. We must live on much more intimate terms with the Chinese gentry, and see far more of their private life than we have hitherto done, before this point can be decided on ; in the mean time, I think it necessary to point out its existence, otherwise the reader might be led to sup-

---

* The Kung family is an exception to this, as it enjoys peculiar privileges.

pose, from the nature of the Chinese institutions, that there can be nothing of the sort here.

A strong proof of the value they set on a pure descent is the nature of the terms of abuse that in the whole empire are considered *most* offensive. In Britain, where as much good faith and honesty exists as in any country of the world, there is, I think, no term that is considered so insufferable as that of *liar*. Englishmen may, in general, be called fools, or by any other abusive epithets, liar excepted, without exciting in them any other emotion than that of contempt, or at the utmost disgust, but this last is almost certain to provoke anger. Now, in China, the most offensive epithets (which are too coarse to be written), though varying in different parts of the empire, all imply impure or illegal parentage.

Many good principles are held up by the Chinese sages for the guidance of man, and even a kind of general sincerity is frequently inculcated, but still a rigid and unswerving adherence to literal truth, which, in all Christian countries forms an important part of the national ethics, and is held in peculiarly high estimation in England, has but little weight laid on it in China. A lie, in itself, is not absolutely criminal in the eyes of a Chinese, and it may, on the contrary, be very meritorious. A Jeannie Deans, far from exciting admiration or sympathy here, would be regarded at best but as a stubborn fanatic. The consequence is, that, although there are, doubtless, individuals to be met with in China who speak the truth and fulfil their promises on all occasions, still, nationally considered, the Chinese are most unscrupulous liars.

Of the domestics, &c., who speak the Canton-English, I say nothing. They, I believe, only tell the truth to foreigners, when they have an especial motive for so doing; when the matter about which they are questioned is indifferent to them, they prefer telling him a lie. They seem, indeed, hitherto to have followed some system of mystification ; doubtless adopted when their numbers were yet small, with the view of retaining the power of cheating the foreigners entirely in their own hands, and partly forced on them by the fear of sharing in the fate of some of their class, who were even put to death by the mandarins for giving information to the foreigners. But I have observed among Chinese who could speak no English, and many of whom had, at the time I met them, never before conversed with foreigners, so much falsehood, that I make it a rule never to trust to what a Chinese says, even on subjects apparently the most indifferent, unless I have some grounds for so doing. What I am told by them, I remember only as something that has been told me, always waiting for corroboration of some kind before giving credence to their tale; and a little acquaintance with the Chinese is sufficient to make most people act thus. Yet the Chinese who have inducements to deceive, when they think their friend is ignorant of the matter in question, or perceive he can scarcely discover the fact with certainty, having no scruples of conscience to make their minds uneasy, lie so unhesitatingly, with such a perfect air of candour, and if doubted, know so well how to assume an appearance of wounded feeling, that the firmest convictions of those who have had most experience of their character, are occasionally apt to be shaken, while those who know little of the people are made to doubt the evidence of their own senses.

The reader, therefore, if he ever have dealings with the Chinese, and would not be duped, must place no reliance on their bare assertions; at the same time, I must particularly warn him against undervaluing them, or treating individuals among them with contempt, on account of this want of veracity. It must be remembered that man does not, when sincerity appears to hurt his own interests, speak the truth naturally, but must be taught to do it by a careful education. Now, as above said, the doctrines of the Chinese sages, though inculcating much morality, lay little or no stress on a rigid adherence to truth, while according to Confucius a lie told by a child to benefit a parent is meritorious. The Christian religion, on the contrary, continually places truth among the virtues, and lying among the lowest vices. By it a lie is *never* praiseworthy; hence we are fully justified in considering a Christian who tells lies as worthless, and capable of any meanness; but we should commit a capital error if we applied the same standard in judging of the Chinese. There are among them as many individuals of high and firm principles, that is to say, of men whom no consideration, not even the fear of death itself, would induce to do what is mean in *their* estimation, as among many, perhaps among any Christian nation. Of this their history contains numberless proofs, which are fully corroborated by a little personal experience of their character. When I, therefore, meet with a Chinese who tells lies and makes false promises, I am no more inclined to regard him as essentially mean by nature, than I would be to regard an Englishman as wicked, who, being married, would "cleave to his wife," and decline paying obedience to commands of his parents interfering with his connubial relations. A refusal to yield obedience to parental commands under these circumstances, in China is considered indicative of a very bad character.

As in every great, busy, and closely connected society, like the Chinese nation, some bond of mutual trust must, however, exist; so we find in China, in the absence of national veracity, of laws compelling the fulfilment of engagements, or the power to put such laws into execution, a custom of *guaranteeing* pervades all domestic and mercantile relations, and even the national institutions, which does much to supply the wants alluded to.   In England we trust a man because we put some confidence in his own honesty, and because we know we can, through the law, obtain redress for breach of trust ; in China people place little or no confidence in each other's honesty, and there is so much uncertainty, difficulty, and even danger, in obtaining redress for breach of trust or contract, by applying to the authorities, that few will venture on an application.   Every Chinese, therefore, who ex- pects to have any kind of trust placed in him, is provided with a guarantee of a standing and respectability sufficient in proportion to the nature and extent of the trust, who, according to the custom, makes himself responsible, in the fullest sense of the word, for any unfaithfulness on the part of the person guaranteed.

It may be objected that the guarantee himself might violate his guaranty ; and at first sight there certainly appears no cause why he should

not.　He is, however, effectually prevented from
this by the power of public opinion.　Every
man, without reflecting deeply on the subject,
feels that some reliable bond of mutual security
is necessary; the guaranty forms, by the general
consent of the nation, that bond in China; and
any man who would venture deliberately to con-
temn it, would lose—what to most people is of
the highest importance—the good opinion of all
classes of society, and the fellowship of his own;
while, even in a pecuniary point of view, he
would probably not be permitted to derive any
benefit from his breach of good faith.　Without,
however, entering farther into causes, I may
state it as a fact, that I have never yet known an
instance of a Chinese openly violating a guaranty
known to have been given by him, and though I
have remarked, that, under strong temptations,
they will sometimes try to evade it, yet instances
of this are extremely rare; and they generally
come promptly forward to meet all the consequences of their responsibility.

The reader, if he come to China, and particularly if he come as a merchant, would do well to
pay particular attention to, and be sure to avail
himself of, the custom just described.　Many of
those who have come here during the last three
years, have suffered from neglecting it.　It is true
that, if your servant runs off with money tempo-

rarily entrusted to him, or a merchant absconds in your debt, the Chinese authorities are bound by the treaties to use all their endeavours to have the criminals sought out and apprehended, and the property recovered. But *the state of a country, and long established customs of a large nation, are not to be altered by treaties;* and, even supposing the mandarins earnestly disposed to act in the cases now alluded to, fully up to the spirit of the treaties, it requires but a slight knowledge of China to perceive that, even then, the person defrauded has but little chance of obtaining redress through them. For any individual, or small number of individuals, to strive against the customs in general of a people is, in reality, as absurd as if they were to oppose a hurricane with hand-bellows; the best plan is, to adapt yourself at once to them. In this particular case, if you deal with well known respectable merchants, they, as it were, guarantee themselves; but in commercial transactions with persons less known, you should be cautious how you give credit without a guaranty. In the same manner all your servants, and others in whom you may be obliged to put trust, should be properly guaranteed. When this is once done, you can place in every respect as much confidence in the Chinese, as in our own countrymen at home, after taking the precautions generally customary there. Should

you, however, notwithstanding your precautions,
be defrauded, you should, on principle, use all the
means placed at your disposal by the treaties to
get the criminal punished, as a warning to others;
but you will save yourself much disappointment
by not expecting to recover your lost property.

It is well known that the Chinese, who are not
forced to it, are by no means fond of bodily exertion; and that the long nails worn by all who can,
are longed for and cultivated, chiefly because they
are a proof that the possessor is not obliged to
perform any hard manual labour. Probably, how-
over, but few of the many who know this, have a
full conception of the extent to which the notions
of the Chinese reach on this point. In England,
where peers of the realm, and commoners with
large hereditary properties, not only hunt, fish,
and shoot, but also take long walks, row, fell
trees, &c. &c., for amusement and exercise; these
employments are, under certain circumstances,
indicative of a person belonging to the higher
classes, and are never considered necessarily
vulgar. The Chinese, however, not only consider
it very extraordinary that rich Europeans should
walk and row, but look on the latter employment
—the only safe exercise the antipathy of the
people permits us beyond the factory squares—as
exceedingly vulgar; and with them it is a strong
proof of the naturally coarse inclinations of the

barbarians. It seems as if many of them—believing, as they do, that England is so small, that if all of us who are abroad and in ships were to return thither, it would scarcely contain us, and that, consequently, a large number of us are born and bred on the water—think we should not be happy unless we got out occasionally on our native element. At all events, far from admiring the manliness of the exercise, they consider the pulling as very vulgar. I, who for obvious reasons am looked upon as civilized to a certain degree, have frequently been remonstrated with, in a delicate manner, on the impropriety of going out in the evening to pull in a gig, when if I *must* go I can engage boatmen to row. And it is to little purpose that I explain the necessity of taking some exercise, and that pulling on the river is somewhat less monotonous than walking up and down a hong, or in one of the factory squares ; to them it appears, that, although reclaimed in some measure, still the force of early habits is too strong, and the barbarian rushes, with ill-concealed delight, to indulge for an hour or two in the propensities of his nature.

The walking puzzles them not a little. Every one who has been at Canton knows, that they will stand for a whole hour, looking at a foreigner walking backwards and forwards, in one of the squares before the factories, their staring eyes fol-

lowing him slowly and regularly, as he passes and
repasses them. They cannot consider it a vulgar
employment, for the lowest Chinese coolie was
never seen walking up and down, without an
apparent object; they have, in consequence, got
several odd notions on the subject; as, that the
foreigner, in his inability to use a swan pan or
abacus, reckons up his accounts in this way; that
it is a religious observance, &c.; and the common
answer to an enquiry made after one thus engaged
is, that he is walking his " thousand steps."

The mandarins, as Chinese, share of course in
the general character of their countrymen; but
among them we remark an unusual degree of
pride, that not unfrequently becomes arrogance.
It should, however, be remembered, that these
men are the élite in point of talent and ability,
in their own extensive and populous country, and
that the pride of conscious merit must be both
greater and more difficult to shake, than that
inspired either by great riches or hereditary rank.
A man may be deprived of his rank and his
riches by his fellow-mortals, but the hand of the
Almighty alone can deprive him of the natural
powers of his mind, and his acquired attainments.
We need, therefore, scarcely be surprised at any
degree of pride on the part of men, who rule both
morally and physically over their fellows, by
virtue of their superior talent, yet humble them-

selves before no God as the giver of it. And,
though the natural talent of the mandarins is,
generally speaking, great, yet having hitherto had
no inducements to make themselves acquainted
with the state of foreign countries, they are as
ignorant of them and as deeply imbued with the
feeling of national superiority as the rest of their
countrymen. The consequence of all this is, that
though among themselves politeness abounds, and
a most marked etiquette is observed, yet among
foreign officers, even those who appear to possess
a natural delicacy of feeling, throw off, without
any affectation, that constraint which is caused by
a respect for our company, while those who are
coarse by nature are apt to be wilfully rude.
Let the British officer fancy himself in company
with a party of Madagascar officials, of different
ranks (several of them, it might be, occupying a
much higher rank in their own country than he
in his); let him suppose himself in such a position, as to have reason to apprehend the personal
consequences if he irritated his associates; let him
fully realize all the contempt he would naturally
feel for the moral attainments of these latter, for
their national institutions, their habits and observances, the impossibility of his really regarding
the highest among them as his superiors, and the
little disposition he would feel to put himself
under constraint, in order to evince a respect he

could not entertain for them ; and he will then be able to form a very correct idea of the feelings of the mandarin, when in company of officers of civilized western nations. This is a point on which I would be understood to speak most positively; for my position, which has given me ample opportunities of observing the conduct of the mandarins, while it does not overawe them by any power attached to it, well enables me to form a judgment. They never, except when driven to it from inability to express themselves otherwise, without giving positive offence, address or speak of foreign officers by the titles and designations used with reference to their own; and it is as galling as it is wholesome for them, to hear the foreigner quietly persist in making that use of them. It is well known that the common designation of foreigners among the people at Canton is *fan kwei,* outlandish devil ; it is used by them precisely as the English use foreigner, or the French, étranger. The mandarins, in like manner, make habitual use of the term *kwei tsï,* devil; which, knowing well it is offensive, they do not indeed employ it before foreigners who understand them ; but it occasionally slips out in the heat of conversation.

If the reader have never left England, or mixed much with foreigners, so as to hear disagreeable truths and untruths, and hence be

most likely accustomed to think of England, and
almost all that is English only, as superior to
every thing else, and as generally admitted to be
so, he will feel highly indignant on reading of
such a state of things as is above described ;
while, even if he be a travelled man, it will require all his cosmopolitism and philanthropy to
enable him to reflect on it without irritation and
a desire to retaliate. And some people who witness it are, indeed, apt to decide that, as the
mandarins, when they think they are not understood, or that the person who hears them dare
not take notice of their language, talk of us
contemptuously, and even behave rudely and
coarsely to us, we ought to treat them in like
manner. But this is a very mistaken notion. It
must be considered, that if they speak and occasionally act thus, it is because they *really* think we
are a coarse, rude people ; now shall we convince
them of the contrary by acting rudely, or perhaps coarsely ? We may by doing so silence
them, and if we go so far as to threaten, or
even to use violence, they may feel fear, or affect
to feel it, in order to appease us ; but they leave
us, not merely believing from report, but thoroughly convinced from their own experience,
that we *are* rude and coarse barbarians. The
proper way to meet them is with steady urbanity ;
in many instances this will put upon their man-

ners those who have just been behaving inso-
lently.   But, as it is a great mistake to submit
to any wilfully prolonged rudeness, if your polite
manner has no effect, then you ought to *explain*,
with perfect equanimity of temper, what it is you
object to, and your reasons for it; and should this
have no effect, you can, according to the circumstances, tell the person, if he persist in his conduct he must leave you or you him; and be sure
to keep your word if he do.   To the last, however, you should be careful not to allow a hasty
word or gesture to escape you.   By such conduct
you may make an insolent Chinese look very
foolish, and cause the witnesses to be very careful
in their behaviour to you.   It is most suited to
the genius of the Chinese, and answers, with the
necessary variations required by station, with all
classes of them.

With respect to the influence Chinese lying
and want of good faith should have on the conduct
of a man who wishes to succeed in his dealings
with them, I will, without troubling the reader
with a statement of reasons, merely say, listen to
their tales, and accept their promises, as if you
really believed the former, and trusted in the
latter, but be careful that you do no such thing;
if you are deceived, lay the blame on your own
simplicity, and, above all things, never evince
indignation.   If you possibly can, preserve, under

all circumstances, an undisturbed manner, express-
ing *nothing* but a placid delight with them and
their society. This is the best way of foiling them,
if they have any secret object in view, for they are
very shrewd, especially the mandarins, at judging
of a man's thoughts and feelings from the expression of his face and his demeanour,—a quality
they acquire, I suppose, from the national want
of veracity obliging them to pay more regard
to each other's faces and manner than to what is
said, in order to ascertain what is meant. By
steadily pursuing the course here recommended—
which, however, is not always an easy task—and
by carefully avoiding all vacillation in your uttered
opinions, and your conduct, you may get on very
well with the Chinese. You will quietly foil their
attempts to gull you, and you will generally gain
any fair object without descending to duplicity,
and without quarrelling.

On the whole, the Chinese are not a disagreeable people to associate with. Their dirty habits
occasion, it is true, a qualm now and then; but
they enjoy a joke, have a great fund of funny
stories, which they can tell well; and urbanity
being decidedly one of their national attributes,
they generally improve as they get better acquainted with the foreigner, and learn to know
what he dislikes, as well as to regard himself and
his country with some respect.

NOTE XVII.

ON THE CHINESE IGNORANCE OF FOREIGN COUN-
TRIES, AND FEELING OF SUPERIORITY OVER
FOREIGNERS.

THERE seems to be an idea now somewhat
prevalent in England, that the Chinese generally
have, in consequence of the late war, attained a
much more correct knowledge of foreigners and
the power and state of their countries than formerly. This is, however, very far from being
the case. Those who saw and felt us, though
sufficient in number to populate a first-rate European kingdom, form but a very small portion of
the Chinese people; and the great body of the
nation, inhabiting districts and provinces that we
have never yet reached, can only look on the late
war as a rebellious irruption of a tribe of barbarians; who, secure in their strong ships, attacked
and took some places along the coast; and even
managed to get into their possession an important
point of the grand canal, whereby they forced
the Emperor to make them certain concessions.
Nearly all they know of the fighting and of the
character of the invading forces they must have

learned from the mandarins' reports to the Emperor, and his answers to them, published in the " Pekin Gazette," and from copies of local proclamations which may have reached them. We may easily imagine, from the tone of these papers, that the Chinese, who, from want of experience, would be unable to form sound judgments on such matters from *correct* data, must entertain opinions on the subject as erroneous as the accounts in these documents are distorted.*

It will be difficult for the Englishman, who is in the habit of obtaining speedy and correct information through the newspapers of all unusual occurrences, not only in his own, but in nearly every country in the world, to comprehend this fully; but he must remember that the Chinese have (with the single exception of the " Pekin Gazette," containing nothing but official documents full of misrepresentations) no newspapers, and that the great body of the nation have no means of learning what passes at a distance from their own township. This is a circumstance which must always be kept in view when reflecting on and drawing conclusions with regard to China and the Chinese, as it accounts for much that will otherwise appear extraordinary.

* The people in and around Canton *now confidently believe* that, although we beat the regular soldiers during the war, their own volunteer corps could expel us from the country.

So much for the nation generally ; as to those who have come, and continue to come into contact with us, let the reader remember how very few foreigners speak Chinese ; that only the Canton and Macao Chinese speak a little English, and that so badly as to be barely intelligible even when speaking of matters relating to their own occupations of tradesmen, mechanics, or menials ;— let the reader recall this to his mind, and he will perceive that, even if the Chinese were eager inquirers into foreign matters, and knew how to put their questions, they must, from the want of opportunity alone, be woefully ignorant of us. But the apathy with respect to foreign things generally, even of the higher and, in the Chinese sense of the word, educated classes, and that when they meet a foreigner who understands their own language, is to an European quite astonishing. They very seldom ask questions, still more seldom is the information they seek after of a kind that tends to enlighten their minds on the state of foreign nations. An intelligent European, accustomed to reflect on the state of a number of countries enjoying a variety of different advantages, and labouring each under peculiar disadvantages, could, by a few well-directed questions, and from very little data, form a tolerably correct notion of the state of a people hitherto unknown to him ; but it would be a great error to suppose that this is the case with the Chinese. Their exclusion of foreigners and confinement to their own country has, by depriving them of all opportunities of making comparisons, sadly circumscribed their ideas; they are thus totally unable to free themselves from the dominion of association, and judge every thing by rules of purely Chinese convention.

If we except one or two of the Chinese officers who have constantly been engaged in the late negotiations with foreigners, and, it may be, a few of those who have had business to transact with the consulates at the five ports, those Chinese who speak the Canton-English, know all that is known of us in China. These people being, as above stated, tradesmen, mechanics, and domestics, are of course nearly all ignorant, in a Chinese point of view; and the following speech of a master carpenter, a man who has probably worked exclusively for foreigners from his youth up, uttered in an unaffected and earnest manner, in the course of a conversation about the building of the British consulate, gives what is by no means an unfair sample of the extent of their information respecting foreign countries. When arguing, not on the state of nations, but on the very business-like subject of work to be done, and the amount of dollars to be given for it, he, in support of some argument, said, " Cuttee outo

Yingkelese king my tingke allo la-che Yingkelese
man savay my ;" i. e. " With the exception of the
Queen (so he meant it) of England, I think all
Englishmen of consequence know me." He had
been in the habit of doing work for the Company's factory, and the idea of the class is that
China, being a large and fertile country, abounding in all good things, while all other places are
small and barren, all our most important possessions must, therefore, lie in China ; hence they
conceive that our head-men, who come here, and
principal merchants, are in fact the chiefs of what
we call our country.

" It is in the great size and wealth and the
numerous population of our country ; still more
in its excellent institutions, which may contain
some imperfections, but which after all are
immeasurably superior to the odd confused rules
by which these barbarians are governed ; but,
above all, in its glorious literature, which contains every noble, elegant, and, in particular,
every profound idea ; every thing, in short, from
which true civilization can spring, that we found
our claim to national superiority." So thinks
even the educated Chinese; and so the whole
nation will continue to think until we have proved
to them—no easy nor short task—our mental as
well as our physical superiority. When some
good works shall have been compiled in Chinese

on natural law, on the principles of political economy, and on European national and international policy, then (after such works shall have obtained a wide circulation) when they perceive how much more deeply metaphysics have been explored by us than by them, and how studiously the best established principles of the sciences included under that term have been brought into practical operation by us, then, but not till then, will the Chinese bow before the *moral* power of the civilized west.

At present they take the tone of superiors quite unaffectedly, simply because they really believe themselves to be superior. I do not remember meeting among educated Chinese with a single instance of any want of candour in regard to this subject; whenever their minds once acknowledge any thing foreign as superior to the Chinese article of the like sort, they at once admit it to be so. For instance, when a mandarin who has never spoken to a barbarian, and never seen one of their books, who, perhaps, has hitherto always doubted that they had any thing deserving of the name, is first shown one, he admires the decided superiority of the paper at once; but when he finds that instead of commencing at the left hand, as it (according to his belief) *of course* ought, its beginning is at the (Chinese) end; when he sees that all the lines, instead of running perpendicularly down the page, in the (to a Chinese) natural way, go sideling across it ; when he further asks the meaning of the words in a sentence, and finds, as may easily happen, that the first comes last, and the last first, " Ah !" says he, without however the slightest intention of giving offence, " it's all confused, I see ; you put the words anywhere, just as it suits your fancy. But how do you manage to read it ?"   When you, however, explain to him at length, that there is no *natural* way for the lines to run, and no absolutely proper place for books to begin; that there can scarcely be said to be any natural order for the succession of words in sentences, but that it is fixed by custom, and differs in every language, and that the uneducated Englishman would consider the Chinese method as quite absurd; when you explain this to him, and he begins to comprehend your reasoning, there is no obstinate *affectation* of contempt.   He cannot, of course, have much respect for the shallow productions of barbarian minds, but he handles the book gravely, no longer regarding it as an absurdity.

All Chinese who have seen them, are perfectly ready to allow, that our ships, our guns, watches, cloths, &c., are much superior to their own articles of the like sort ; and most of them would frankly admit us to be superior to them in all respects, if they thought so. But, as above said, they do not. They are quite unable to draw conclusions as to the state of foreign countries, from an inspection of the articles produced or manufactured in them. They cannot see that a country where such an enormous, yet beautiful fabric as a large English ship is constructed—an operation requiring at once the united efforts of numbers, and a high degree of skill—*must* be inhabited by a people, not only energetic, but rich and free to enjoy the fruits of its own labour ; that such a country *must,* in short, have a powerful government, good laws, and be altogether in a high stage of civilization. All this the Chinaman, having never compared the various states of different nations, is not only quite unable to perceive of himself, but often not even when it is pointed out to him at great length. We have, it is true, the power to do some great and extraordinary things, but so have the elephants and other wild animals, he occasionally sees and hears of ; in his eyes, therefore, we are all barbarians, possessing perhaps some good qualities, congregated perhaps together in some sort of societies, but without regular government, untutored, coarse, and wild.

NOTE XVIII.

I WAS led to notice this subject by the perusal
of an American pamphlet, entitled " Remarks on
China, and the China Trade," by R. B. Forbes:
Boston, 1844 ; and in particular, by the following
paragraph it contains :—

" All the spare *cash* to be had in China is
needed to pay for the opium, grown under the
auspices of the government of Great Britain,
and under the immediate superintendence of the
servants of the Honourable East India Company.
Could the opium trade be abolished, there is no
doubt that a compensation would be found in
the increased sale of manufactured goods, because
there would be more ready cash, and more industry in the country to pay for them."

From this passage, taken in connection with
the tone of the whole pamphlet, the writer
seems to think, that if the East India Company
prohibited the growth of opium in its territories,
less money would be exported from China in
exchange for opium.

Now he says that he "has been long engaged in the China trade" himself, but notwithstanding the advantages he must thus have possessed for obtaining good information, it seems easy to prove that he makes a prediction than which nothing could be more false, or in other words, that the *very reverse* of what he predicts would really ensue. Whoever has paid any attention to opium smokers will have perceived, that even those who use the drug in moderation, suffer very much if they are prevented from taking it at their usual time, that their sufferings increase as the duration of the abstinence is prolonged, and become at length really fearful. It is consequently evident, that even such moderate smokers would be forced to give up all their money, and sacrifice every comfort they might possess to obtain opium, should any occurrence, as for instance a rise in its price, reduce them to such steps in order to procure it.

Now what would, under these circumstances, be the consequence, if the growth of opium were suddenly prohibited in British India? All the stock then already existing, and all the supplies from the other places where it may now be grown, as Turkey, would be bought up at an exorbitant price; the Chinaman, who now smokes about one-sixth of an ounce per diem,* and pays

* A very great number of Chinese, men who attend with

twelve cents for it, would then be reduced to impoverish himself and his family, in order to procure a very insufficient allowance ; what is the case with one smoker would be the case with all —at least with all to whom the use of opium has become indispensable, i. e. *with all those whose present outlay for it is so great, as perceptibly to increase the scarcity of money for other purposes,* —and the evident consequence would be, that until the old quantity could be obtained from the new places of growth which would rapidly spring into existence—until that time the " cash " laid out for opium would amount to a much greater sum than is now expended on it, and numbers of Chinese families would be reduced to beggary, as also numbers of Indian natives now employed in the cultivation and preparation of the article. Therefore, the more opium is grown, either under, or independent of " the immediate sur- veillance of the Honourable East India Com- pany," the better is it at the present moment for the interest of the manufacturers in England and America.

As to the Chinese government putting down the use of opium by prohibitory measures, even if assisted by a cordial quixotic co-operation on

the greatest punctuality to their daily business, and support themselves and their families in a decent manner, consume about the quantity daily.

the part of England, it requires such a slight
knowledge of the state of things here to see
the impossibility of success in such an attempt,
that it is unnecessary to say any thing on the
point to the readers for whom these Notes are
chiefly intended.

The use of opium in China to a certain extent
will never cease ; but it might in time be confined
to the most degraded of the people : and in
particular the comparative amount of bullion
materially reduced, which its consumption causes
to be expended in a manner directly baneful
to China, and infinitely less beneficial to us than
its outlay in comforts, or innoxious luxuries in
the shape of manufactures would be.

The adoption of plans which have frequently
been recommended for the attainment of somewhat different objects, would gradually procure
these two results ; the truth of which assertion
will, I trust, become plain, if we view the working
of these plans in connection as one.   It would
then be simply this ; to prevail on the Chinese
government to annul its prohibitions against the
growth of the opium, and permit its importation
free of all duty; and to get the East India
Company to take such steps as would, without
injuring its revenue, render the drug cheaper
in China.

If a plan that is proposed to effect any great

purpose be of a violent nature, and consequently run directly counter to the wishes of
certain classes, we have, for that reason alone,
good right to suspect its feasibility, no matter
how well adapted it may otherwise seem to
attain the object in view, or how laudable soever
that object may be. Such plans are almost
certain to entail evils, the occurrence of which
was never even contemplated by their devisers.
Witness the forcible suppression of the slave
trade on the coast of Africa; which has caused
the slaves to suffer more than ever in their
transportation across the Atlantic; has frequently caused the deliberate murder of an
entire cargo; has kept us in constant bickerings
with the French and Americans, about the right
of search; has even induced the latter to refuse
this right to a degree likely to encourage piracy;
and which, if I may judge from the public papers,
is extremely likely to furnish the first grounds
for a bitter. war between us and one or both of
the above-named nations. Witness, too, Napoleon's attempt to ruin England by such a violent
method as the prohibition of her manufactures
and colonial produce on the Continent; which,
without accomplishing the purpose he had in
view, materially tended (no *evil* indeed) to render
the overthrow of his power decisive, by making
it an object of earnest desire to every one in the

states he controlled, down to the old peasant woman in Germany, who was, by this measure obliged to give up coffee altogether, and take *nothing but* chicory.

Now, the plan here recommended is in so far perfectly unobjectionable, that it runs counter to the wishes of no one, with the exception, perhaps, of a few Chinese smugglers, who by its adoption simply would be deprived of the tie that makes them a class, and would, therefore, soon cease to exist. It would be welcomed by all others engaged in the production of, and trade in, the article ; and, what is of most consequence, it would in particular be highly agreeable to the consumers, the class upon whose good wishes, more than those of either the present producers or carriers, must be based every sound plan intended to effect a great commercial change.

To every one acquainted with the history of mankind, from the days of Eve downwards, or who has studied the motives by which human beings are actuated, one of the effects that would result from annulling the prohibitions against opium will be at once apparent. The opium smoking would lose that charm which allures man to do what is forbidden, merely because it is so ; a strange charm, which operates so powerfully, that were gin prohibited in England, with the view of benefitting the wretched classes

R

who now form its principal consumers, it may be unhesitatingly asserted, that even in England—where laws, if any where, can be enforced—it would soon become an article of common use among the middle and higher classes, who now scarcely ever see it.

Another effect of abolishing the prohibitions would, of course, be to render the drug cheaper, even were other things to remain as before; since that part of the price, which now serves to remunerate the smuggler and dealer for the risks they run, would then disappear. Now, to render it cheaper, and thus less a luxury and less recherché, is the most essential part of the plan: for all my inquiries convince me, that people commence smoking opium in China as soon as their means permit them, chiefly because it is thought rather a fine thing; just as many young men commence cigar smoking in England.

No duty should be charged on it when imported, and that for two reasons; first, because, as just stated, it is a part of the plan to render the drug cheap; and secondly, because any attempt to increase the Chinese revenue by an opium duty would be very unpopular among the Chinese who do not use it. It would by them be regarded as a trifling on the part of the Emperor with the welfare of his subjects, out of purely selfish motives: and, as things are constituted in China, could not fail to degrade and weaken the Imperial government. And here (to anticipate those who persist in basing their arguments against any plan on the perverted views their prejudices cause them to take of it) I would observe, that the present one does *not*, by any means, render it necessary that the use of the opium should be countenanced by the Imperial government. It should, on the contrary, steadily discountenance it, by dismissing from service all new officials, and stopping the promotion of all old ones, addicted to it. This should, however, not be done on any abstract grounds of morality (how many have become drunkards in Christian countries, merely because drunkenness is decried by serious people as immoral!), but on the cold practical one of incapacity for business on the part of those who indulge in it to any extent. There is a sort of pleasure to young folks, in turning a heedless ear to the disinterested and anxious admonitions of superiors and elders; but when the latter manifest a perfect indifference to the personal welfare of these same young people, the greater part soon find it necessary to attend earnestly to that interesting subject themselves.

When the opium had lost the charm of prohibition and costliness, the folly of using such a pernicious drug would soon become glaring to a reasoning and generally sober people like the

Chinese, especially if its use were made a bar to official employment ; this, in all other countries eagerly sought after, as the *chief* road to distinction, being in China still more an object of desire as the *only* one.

The full adoption by the East India Company, and by the Imperial government at the instance of foreign states, of the measures which constitute this plan, would undoubtedly bring about, as an immediate consequence, a temporary increase in the consumption of opium ; and probably both the present and the next succeeding generation would pass before its beneficial effects would generally manifest themselves. This period will seem long in the eyes of western philanthropists ; but those among them who will take the trouble to acquaint themselves with the real nature of the abuse, with the history of its progress and present extent, and then set to work devising and canvassing the merits of other plans for cutting it off, will soon perceive that any such other plan would only tend to procrastinate its abatement still longer, and (judging by analogy) would induce evils of which no one has at present the remotest conception. The opium smoking must itself work its own cure. Like an immense body of confined water which has, unheeded, gradually worked itself an outlet so great that human force can no longer stop the torrent

rushing from it, so the opium flood is now
pouring into China a high and compact stream,
which defies all resistance, and overwhelms every
every one in its course ; and it will not lose its
destroying power until it has weakened itself
by spreading out over the whole face of the
country.

NOTE XIX.

APPLICATION OF THE CONCLUSION ARRIVED AT IN
NOTE XI. TO THE POLICY AND PROSPECTS OF
OUR OWN COUNTRY.

At the end of Note XI. I have said that China
forms a practical lesson for the rulers of all other
states ; and with this practical lesson constantly
under my eyes, I find it impossible to close without making a short digression to point out one,
at least, of the effects that would result from the
adoption of the Chinese grand principle of government by our rulers.

England will certainly lose every colony she
possesses unless she adopts some system of impartial elevation of colonists to the posts and
honours at the disposal of the crown ; and she
will then become a secondary power in comparison with states of larger territory and greater
resources, as the United States of North America, as Russia, and as the larger of her present
colonies, when the one and the other shall have
increased in population and wealth : she will sink
to a secondary power before these, just as Holland

has sunk before her, notwithstanding the industry and enterprise, the patriotic bravery, and the unparalleled exertions of the Dutch nation, as well as its unexampled wealth and maritime greatness at the time the struggle commenced. The injustice of making colonists contribute to honours in which they have no participation, and pay for a set of rulers in whom they have no interest, in whom, too, they will not fail to discover a latent assumption of personal superiority; the injustice of this is too glaring and too aggravating. And the (consequently) natural anti-government spirit already plainly perceptible in every British colony, having nothing whatever to counteract its increase, will at length display itself in their employing the means at present so expended, to the honour and profit of their own people, and in their shaking off all connection with the mother country. They will then not only cease to take the slightest interest in her welfare, but will gradually become her most embittered and dangerous enemies.

Let, on the contrary, the colonists feel that they virtually possess every advantage and privilege of British subjects; that notwithstanding their greater distance from the central government, they have a chance of rising, and of enjoying the honours of the empire *equal* to that of the younger branches of the most influential families

in England ; let them see and hear of their sons
as civilians, as members of the judicial body, as
military and naval officers, not only in their native colonies, but distributed throughout all the
others as well as in the mother country; let this
be done *systematically, and in a manner of the impartiality of which there can be no doubt, without
which they will not appear as candidates ;* let us, in
short, cease to hear of the dependence, and learn
to know only the participation of the colonies,
and England maintains for ever her high position
among the most powerful countries of the world.

It is no exaggeration to say, that the constant
gratification of the deepest, and most universally
felt passion of human nature, and the greater
degree in which this passion can be gratified, as
well as every other social and national advantage
enjoyed by the members of an immense empire,
would not only render a separation from the
mother country no object of desire, but would
make it a most severely felt punishment to any
individual colony.   It would urge each of them
to join itself more closely to her, and through her
to the rest of the colonies ; and it is well to
remember, that our North American possessions
are now as near to London, as Scotland was *at
the union of the parliaments ;* and further, that the
increased rapidity of communication, which is
certain to take place, will bring some succeeding

generation of our antipodean colonies in Australia as near as the present one of the Canadas.

Some well-digested system of local and metropolitan general examinations, for all British subjects, like that which has existed with little variation in China for the last thousand years, but in more useful matters, and followed by *special* metropolitan examinations, to be passed before admission to the various subdivisions of the three branches of the executive ;—some system like this would most effectually secure that impartiality, without which the desired object would not be gained ; and it would, at the same time, bring about a perfect similarity of language, and a consequent unity of feeling throughout the empire, which cannot easily be over-valued.

The measure I have recommended would not, however, stop short in its operation at the cementing of a close union between England and her colonies. In the British empire, juries, a parliament, and a free press, afford the means of ensuring a greater impartiality in the examinations than can be attained with every precaution in China ; and prevent of themselves many evils, that must here be counterbalanced by the (in so far unproductive, though useful) operation of the principle on which the examinations are founded ; hence it is difficult to foresee all the beneficial effects which the adoption of this measure would

s

produce. But we can, at all events, perceive that
it would excite an extraordinary spirit of emulation, both in the mother country and the colonies ;
that it would gradually diffuse sound information
among all classes, to an extent, and with an
economy, no other plan of promoting national
education will insure ; and that it would secure
to the crown a body of intelligent and able
servants. And we might, in short, confidently
expect from it all the vast benefits which must
infallibly result from a grand national measure,
based on strict justice,—on that unerring righte-
ousness, which we are told "EXALTETH NATIONS,"
and "ESTABLISHETH THRONES."

FINIS.

Lightning Source UK Ltd.
Milton Keynes UK
UKOW04f1416110917
308978UK00001B/4/P